Compendium Volume Eight

To

Commentary

on

The Book of Mormon

Philip M. Hudson

"A mind that has been stretched by a new idea can never return to its original dimension." (Oliver Wendell Holmes).

Copyright 2024 by Philip M. Hudson.
Published 2024.
Printed in the United States of America.
All rights reserved.

No portion of this book may be reproduced,
stored in a retrieval system, or transmitted
in any form or by any means, mechanical,
electronic, photocopy, recording, scanning,
or other, except for brief quotations in
critical reviews or articles, without
the prior written permission
of the author.

ISBN 978-1-957077-81-9
Illustrations - Google Images.

This book may be ordered from
online bookstores.

Publishing Services
by BookCrafters, Parker, Colorado.
www.bookcrafters.net

The worth of principles is validated
by our witness, or our testimony. The Book of
Mormon emphasizes that baptism is the outward
expression of our personal dedication to obedience.
It is the public manifestation of our desire to
have a private covenant relationship with
God. It is the voluntary surrender of
our agency to a higher power,
the subjugation of our
desires to His
will.

Index to Compendia Volumes 3-7

Every
Nephite family
that was created thru
the power and authority of
God became another of the basic
building blocks of eternity. Today,
the Church of Jesus Christ emphasizes
the worth of the family, and it is held in
the highest esteem. It regards the family as
a definitive expression of individuality,
creativity, and interdependence. But
more than that, it is the tangible
expression of God's glory.
(See Moses 1:39).

Volume 3 Essays

Abstinence in a Permissive World
Additional Scripture
Addressing Deity
Agency
Agency and Opposition
Agency and Youth
Age of Accountability
Alma's Discourse on Faith
And it Came to Pass
And Thus We See
Angels
Are Mormons Christian?
Are We Alone in The Universe?
(The) Atonement
Bah Humbug!
Baptism
Batteries are Not Included
Become as Little Children
Before a Wound Can Heal
Behold
Being Well Grounded
(The) Bible
(The) Biggest Loser
Blood, Covenant, and Land Israel
(The) Book of Mormon as History
Book of Mormon Strengths

(The) Book of Mormon was Preserved for our Day
Born Again Christians
Brevity)
Buddy Can You Spare a Dime?
Caesar
(A) Change of Heart
(The) Character of God
Choose the Harder Right
Choose ye This Day
Christians
(A) Christmas Miracle
Christ's Church is Restored
(The) Church
(The) Church of Jesus Christ in Former Times
Circle of Knowledge
Citizenship in The Church and Kingdom
Civil Liberties
(A) Coat of Many Colors
Cogito Ergo Sum
Cognates in The Book of Mormon
Combatting Evil
Commitment
Conditional Sentences in The Book of Mormon
Connections
Construction Zone: Proceed with Caution
Conversion

It
must have been
the wish of every of
the Nephite prophets that
the Savior would not send
a famine into the land, but
instead grant that their people
might live in Bethlehem. They
knew that the habitation of the
Lord was as a house of bread
where the faithful could go
to partake of His word,
that was the true
staff of life.

Volume 4 Essays

Courage
Covenant Consciousness
Covenants
(The) Creation of The World
Dancing With the Stars
(The) Desert Shall Rejoice
Diversity
Doctrine – The Meaning of
(The) Door Swings Both Ways
Dry Humor in The Book of Mormon
(The) Dust of The Earth
(The) Duty of The Priest
Education
(The Best) Education
Enduring to The End
Entropy in The Physical and Eternal Worlds
Environmental Concerns: An Eternal Perspective
Establishing the Word
(Our) Eternal Nature
Eternal Progression in a Dynamic Universe
Everyone Wants to Go to Heaven
Evidences of God
Faith and Knowledge
Faith Building

Faith is a Principle of Power
(The) Fall
Fasting
Fate
Father Forgive Them
Finding Balance in Our Lives
Friendship
Focus
Follow the Prophet
Forgiveness
For Unto Us a Child is Born
(The Importance of) Friends
Friendship
Gathering of Israel
General Conference
(The) Germination of our Faith
Gifts of The Spirit
God is NowHere
Godly Qualities
God's Tactical Flashlight
Gold – The Appearance of
Grace
Gratitude

Happiness, it seems, is like a butterfly. (See 2 Nephi 5:27). The more we chase it, the more it will elude us. But if we turn our attention to selfless acts and service in behalf of others, it will come and rest quietly on our shoulder. (Anonymous).

Volume 5 Essays

Happiness
Happiness and Sharing the Gospel
Happiness / Wickedness
Having Been Commissioned of Jesus Christ
Heaven Can Wait
Heavenly Father Knows Us
(The) Heavens Were Opened
Higher Dimensional Realities
(The) Holy Ghost
(The) Holy Grail of Religious Doctrine
Honesty
(The) Hourglass of Life
How Does God Get Things Done?
Huckleberries and Chokeberries
Humility
Hypocrisy
I am a Child of God
I Have Fought a Good Fight
I Have Overcome the World
Isaiah in The Book of Mormon
Is Heaven Hotter Than Hell?
It's Our Book
Joseph Smith: A Rough Stone Rolling
Joseph Smith History
Joseph Smith's World

Jumping Out of Our Skin
Just Get Back on The Bike
Justice
Justice and Mercy
Keep Smiling
Labels
Lamanites by The Waters of Sebus
(The) Last Judgment
Life is a Three Act Play
Life or Death?
Life's Greatest Questions
Life's Important Decisions
Light
Light and Darkness
Light and Truth
(The) Light of Christ
(The) Light of The World
Limiting Beliefs
Living Water
Look Who's Coming to Town
Lost Books of The Bible
(The) Lost Manuscript
(The) Lost Ten Tribes
Lucifer

When they were just
eight years old, Nephite children
received the ordinance of baptism and
entered in at the strait gate. The way was
narrowly defined and invited their little
ones to be immersed as soon as they had
arrived at the age of accountability,
and then to receive the gift of the
Holy Ghost. For it was by both
water and the Spirit that
they were sanctified
to enjoy God's
gifts.

Volume 6 Essays

- (A) Mailbox Marked With an "X"
- Management by The Spirit
- (The) Manifestation of Spirits
- May the 4th Be With You
- (The) Millennium
- (The) Mind of God
- Missing Scripture
- Missionary Work
- Moral Discipline
- Mothers
- Multi-tasking
- (The) Name of Christ in The Book of Mormon
- (The) Nature of God and Our Covenants
- (Our) Neighbors
- No Greater Call
- (The) Number of Disciples Was Multiplied
- Obedience
- One Lord, One Faith, One Baptism
- Persecution
- Personal Revelation
- (The) Plan of Salvation
- (The) Plan of Salvation 15 Names
- (A) Positive Mental Attitude
- Power: The Ultimate Test of Character
- Pragmatism in The Book of Mormon
- Premortal Life
- Preparation
- Pride
- (The) Priests of Baal in Our Lives
- (The) Prime Directive
- Professors
- Proper Prior Preparation
- (The) Prophet Joseph Smith
- Prophet, Seer, and
- (The) Q Continuum
- Quorum Sensing
- Receiving Revelation
- Recognizing the Church of Christ
- Removing the Barnacles of Life
- Restoration – The Early Days
- Revelation
- Reverence
- (The) Sabbath
- (The) Sacrament
- Sacramental Waters
- Satan
- (The) Scope of Our Decisions
- (The) Second Mile
- Service
- Set Apart
- Sharing the Gospel
- Sharper Than a Two-edged Sword
- (The) Sons of Mosiah
- Speak Kind Words to Each Other
- (The) Spirit of Revelation

In the best
of times, the Nephites
consecrated their behavior
that they might secure both
the blessings and benedictions
of celestial glories, to be destined
to reign as kings and priests, and
queens and priestesses, to become
joint heirs of dominions whose
reach would be bound only
by the holy Order
of the Son of
God.

Volume 7 Essays

Spiritual Calisthenics
Spiritual Gifts
Spiritual Identity Theft
(A) Standard of Excellence
Strangers in The Land
Strengths and Weaknesses
Studying the Scriptures
Success Strategies
Symbols
Talents
Teaching in The Church
Teaching Key Doctrine
Technological Traps
(A) Testimony of Christ
(A) Thirty Day Spiritual Fitness Program
Thou Hast Done Wonderful Things
(The) Thrill of Victory / Agony of DeFeet
Tithing
Too Good to Be True
(The) Tools of The Trade

Touching His Garment
Tough Questions
Travel at The Speed of Thought
(The) Twelve Tribes of Israel
Types, Rites, Ceremonies, and Symbols (Alma Unity
Updates are Ready
Walk in The Light of The Lord
(Our) Weaknesses
Were There Two Cumorahs?
What Think Ye of Christ?
Wherefore and Therefore in The Book of Mormon
(A) Whirlwind into Heaven
Who is Packing Your Parachute?
Why We Laugh
Words of Mormon
Work and Personal Responsibility
Worship in Music
Writing on Metal Plates Was a Pain
Zion

"Sometimes, during solitude, the Nephites heard truth spoken with clarity and freshness. Uncolored and untranslated, it spoke from within themselves in a language that was original but inarticulate, heard only with the soul, and they realized they brought it with them, were never taught it, nor could they efficiently teach it to others."
(Hugh B. Brown).

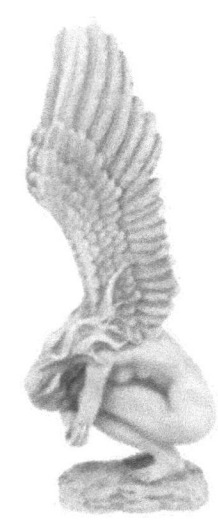

Compendium Volume 3-7 Scriptures

Introduction - Look Who's Coming to Town
1 Nephi 1:20 - Follow the Prophet
2 Nephi 1:30 - Friendship
1 Nephi 2:1-3 - Life's Important Decisions
1 Nephi 3:7 - Obedience
1 Nephi 3:15-16 - Just Get Back on The Bike
1 Nephi 8:2 - Cognates in The Book of Mormon
1 Nephi 8:20 – (The) Hourglass of Life
1 Nephi 8:24 & 11:25 - Being Well Grounded
1 Nephi 9:5-6 – (The) Lost Manuscript
1 Nephi 11:6 & 8 - Jumping Out of Our Skin
1 Nephi 11:25 - Living Water
1 Nephi 13:26 - (The) Lost Books of The Bible
1 Nephi 14:7 - Book of Mormon Strengths
1 Nephi 14:10 – (The) Church
1 Nephi 15:14 - Teaching Key Doctrine
1 Nephi 15:20 - Gathering of Israel
1 Nephi 15:30 - God's Tactical Flashlight
1 Nephi 17:22 - Speak Kind Words
1 Nephi 17:50-51 - Multi-tasking
1 Nephi 19:12 - Environmental Concerns
1 Nephi 20:6 - Circle of Knowledge
1 Nephi 21:25 - Combatting Evil
2 Nephi 1:30 - Friendship
2 Nephi 2:4 – (The) Fall
2 Nephi 2:11 - Entropy
2 Nephi 2:15-16) - Work & Responsibility
2 Nephi 2:16 & 27 – Agency
2 Nephi 2:2 &, Alma 42:8 - Why We Laugh
2 Nephi 2:27 - Fate
2 Nephi 2:28 - Cogito Ergo Sum
2 Nephi 3:7 - Joseph Smith: A Rough Stone
2 Nephi 3:7 & 15 – (The)Prophet Joseph Smith
2 Nephi 31:16 & 18, & Moroni 10:5 - Joseph Smith

2 Nephi 4:35 - Life's Greatest Questions
2 Nephi 9:13 - Plan of Salvation Names
2 Nephi 9:13 - Holy Grail of Religious Doctrine
2 Nephi 9:18 – (The) Church in Former Times
2 Nephi 9:29 - Agency and Opposition
2 Nephi 9:29 - Education
2 Nephi 11:7 - (The) Creation of The World
2 Nephi 12:5 - Walk in The Light
2 Nephi 15:20 - Light and Darkness
2 Nephi 21:6-9 – (The) Millennium
2 Nephi 21:22-23 – (The) Desert Shall Rejoice
2 Nephi 21:31 - Quorum Sensing
2 Nephi 21:31 - (The Meaning of) Doctrine
2 Nephi 24:1 - Strangers in The Land
2 Nephi 24:12 - Lucifer
2 Nephi 25:23 - Grace
2 Nephi 25:1 - Are Mormons Christian?
2 Nephi 26:14 - (The) Church in The Last Days
2 Nephi 26:16 - Book of Mormon Preserved
2 Nephi 26:16 - Establishing the Word
2 Nephi 26:29 – (The) Priests of Baal
2 Nephi 27:10-11 - Receiving Revelation
2 Nephi 27:26 – Wonderful Things
2 Nephi 28:3-4 - (The Best) Education
2 Nephi 28:12 - Pride
2 Nephi 28:20 - God is NowHere
2 Nephi 28:26 - Power: Ultimate Test of Character
2 Nephi 28:30 - Christ's Church is Restored
2 Nephi 28:30-32 - Updates are Ready
2 Nephi 29:3 – (The) Bible
2 Nephi 29:6 - For Unto Us a Child is Born
2 Nephi 29:7-8 - Additional Scripture
2 Nephi 30:2 & 2 Nephi 24:1-2 - Blood, Covenant, and Land Israel

The Law was not written with ink, nor on paper with pen, but within the hearts of the Nephites. In the best of times, it unerringly guided their actions. Without conscious effort on their part, they held securely to the rod of iron, for they intuitively knew it to be true. It had been stitched into their sinews by the power of the Holy Ghost.

2 Nephi 31:16 & 18, & Moroni 10:5 - Joseph Smith History
2 Nephi 31:17-18 - Eternal Progression
2 Nephi 31:19-20 - (The) Prime Directive
2 Nephi 31:20 - Spiritual Calisthenics
2 Nephi 32:5-6 - Faith and Knowledge
2 Nephi 33:4 – (The) Second Mile
Jacob 1:6 - Revelation
Jacob 1:13-14 – (Our) Neighbors
Jacob 2:31 - Abstinence in a Permissive World
Jacob 4:6 – (The Spirit of) Revelation
Jacob 4:8 – (The) Mind of God
Jacob 4:11 - Faith Building
Jacob 4:13 - Too Good to Be True
Jacob 5:10 - Is Heaven Hotter Than Hell?
Enos 1:27 - Spiritual Identity Theft
Jarom 1:4 - Godly Qualities
Jarom 1:5 – (The) Sabbath
Jarom 1:20 - Plan of Salvation
Omni 1:26 - Fasting
Words of Mormon 1:3 - Words of Mormon
Words of Mormon 1:5 - Brevity
Mosiah 2:1 - General Conference
Mosiah 2:17 - Service
Mosiah 2:25 – (The) Dust of The Earth
Mosiah 3:12-13 - Proper Prior Preparation
Mosiah 3:15 - Symbols
Mosiah 3:19 – (The) Atonement
Mosiah 4:9 - Are We Alone in The Universe?
Mosiah 4:19 - Buddy Can You Spare a Dime?)
Mosiah 4:20-21 - Batteries are Not Included
Mosiah 4:27 - Finding Balance in Our Lives
Mosiah 5:7 - I am a Child of God
Mosiah 5:7 - Born Again Christians
Mosiah 5:7 - A Change of Heart
Mosiah 5:8-10 - Huckleberries and Chokeberries
Mosiah 8:13 & 16-17 – Heavens Were Opened
Mosiah 8:16 - Prophet, Seer, and
Mosiah 15:14-18 – (The) Thrill of Victory &
   The Agony of DeFeet
Mosiah 18:20 - Before a Wound Can Heal
Mosiah 18:21 – (A) Positive Mental Attitude
Mosiah 23:16-17 & 25:29 - Having Been
   Commissioned of Jesus Christ
Mosiah 25:19-20 – (The) Duty of The Priest

Mosiah 26:22 - Father Forgive Them
Mosiah 27:3 - Teaching in The Church
Mosiah 27:8-9 - Agency and Youth
Mosiah 27:11 - Angels
Mosiah 29:2 - Caesar
Mosiah 29:12-13 - Citizenship
Alma 5:7 - Set Apart
Alma 5:26 - Worship in Music
Alma 5:46 - Personal Revelation
Alma 7:20 - How Does God Get Things Done?
Alma 9:19-23 - Talents
Alma 11:43 – (The) Biggest Loser
Alma 12:27 – (The) Last Judgment
Alma 13:3 - Life is a Three Act Play
Alma 13:3 - Premortal Life
Alma 17:2-3 – (The) Sons of Mosiah
Alma 17:4 - Sharing the Gospel
Alma 17:34-36 – Lamanites by The Waters of Sebus
Alma 22:18 - Removing the Barnacles of Life
Alma 26:8 - Gratitude
Alma 27:27 - Honesty
Alma 26:23-24 – (The) Scope of Our Decisions
Alma 29:1 - Happiness and Sharing the Gospel
Alma 29:1-2 - No Greater Call
Alma 29:4 - Life or Death?
Alma 30:7-9 - Choose Ye This Day
Alma 30:13 - Everyone Wants to Go to Heaven
Alma 30:13 - Evidences of God
Alma 30:41 – (A) Testimony of Christ
Alma 30:44 - Dancing With the Stars
Alma 31:5 - Studying the Scriptures
Alma 31:5 - (Spiritual Fitness Program
Alma 32:5 - Limiting Beliefs
Alma 32:27 - Alma's Discourse on Faith
Alma 32:28 – (The) Germination of Our Faith
Alma 32:35 - Light
Alma 32:42-43 – (The) Tools of The Trade
Alma 34:32 - Preparation
Alma 36:12-14 - Bah Humbug!
Alma 36:19 - I Have Overcome the World
Alma 37:45 - Types, Rites, Ceremonies,
   and Symbols
Alma 40:20 - Construction Zone

Samuel was
a humble servant of the Lord
who preached faith and repentance.
Offering the ordinances of baptism and
the Holy Ghost, he taught the gospel to a society
that was dying of spiritual thirst. There were among
his listeners in Zarahemla a few repentant guilty who
had wandered across the deserts of Idumea. (See Helaman
15:13). They sought the cleansing waters of redemption,
and longed for the healing balm of Gilead promised by
the prophet, who would be a savior on Mount Zion,
who was prepared to reveal to their open hearts
the certain knowledge of the love and
concern of their Father Who
dwelt in heaven.

Alma 40:23-24 – (Our) Eternal Nature
Alma 41:10 - Happiness
Alma 41:13 - Justice
Alma 42:13-15 - Justice and Mercy
Alma 42:26 – (The) Character of God
Alma 46:12 - A Coat of Many Colors
Alma 46:15 - Christians
Alma 46:20 - May the 4th Be With You
Alma 48:7 - Courage
Alma 48:19 - Choose the Harder Right
Alms 50:23 - Happiness / Wickedness
Alma 51:5-6 - Civil Liberties
Alma 56:47-48 - Mothers
Alma 60:6-7 - Focus
Helaman 3:25-28 - The Number of Disciples Was Multiplied
Helaman 3:33 - Professors
Helaman 3:35 - Touching His Garment
Helaman 3:35 - Humility
Helaman 5:12 - Covenant Consciousness
Helaman 6:37 - Missionary Work
Helaman 10:6 - Heavenly Father Knows Us
Helaman 12:7-10 - Sharper Than a Two-edged Sword
Helaman 16:23 - Satan
Helaman 18:19-20 - Missing Scripture
Helaman 13:38 - Heaven Can Wait
3 Nephi 1:12-13 - (A) Christmas Miracle
3 Nephi 9:33 - Conversion
3 Nephi 11:10-11 – (The) Light of the World
3 Nephi 12:2 - What Think Ye of Christ?
3 Nephi 12:10 - Persecution
3 Nephi 12:48 - Nature of God and Covenants
3 Nephi 13:9 - Addressing Deity
3 Nephi 13:14 - Forgiveness
3 Nephi 13:14-15 – Door Swings Both Ways
3 Nephi 13:22 - (The) Q Continuum
3 Nephi 14:5 - Hypocrisy
3 Nephi 14:11 - Spiritual Gifts
3 Nephi 14:22-23 – (A) Mailbox Marked With an "X"
3 Nephi 15:9 - Enduring to The End
3 Nephi 16:1-3 – (The) Twelve Tribes of Israel
3 Nephi 17:4 – (The) Lost Ten Tribes
3 Nephi 19:30 - Keep Smiling
3 Nephi 23:1 - Isaiah in The Book of Mormon

3 Nephi 24:8-10 - Tithing
3 Nephi 26:14 - Become as Little Children
3 Nephi 27:5 - (The) Name of Christ in The Book of Mormon
3 Nephi 27:8 – Recognizing the Church of Christ
3 Nephi 27:13-20 - Baptism
3 Nephi 27:22 - Restoration, The Early Days
3 Nephi 27:28-29 - Tough Questions
3 Nephi 28:6 - Travel at The Speed of Thought
3 Nephi 28:13-15 – Higher Dimensional Realities
3 Nephi 28:13-15 – (A) Whirlwind into Heaven
3 Nephi 29:3 - Covenants
4 Nephi 1:17 - Labels
4 Nephi 1:17-18 - Unity
Mormon 1:3-4 – Book of Mormon as History
Mormon 3:20-22 - It's Our Book
Mormon 6:2 - Were There Two Cumorahs?
Mormon 8:5 – (The Importance of) Friends
Mormon 8:8 - Age of Accountability
Mormon 8:35 - Connections
Mormon 8:35 - Joseph Smith's World
Mormon 8:38 - (Our) Neighbors
Mormon 8:38 - Technological Traps
Mormon 9:6 - Who is Packing Your Parachute?
Mormon 9:32-33 - And it Came to Pass
Ether 4:12 - Light and Truth
Ether 12:24-25, Jacob 4:1 & Mormon 8:17 - Writing on Metal Plates Was a Pain
Ether 12:26 – (Our) Weaknesses
Ether 12:27 - Strengths and Weaknesses
Ether 15:11 - Gold – The Appearance of
Moroni 2:2 - (The) Holy Ghost
Moroni 4:1 - (The) Sacrament
Moroni 5:1-2 - Sacramental Waters
Moroni 6:9 - Reverence
Moroni 7:13 - Management by The Spirit
Moroni 7:19 – (The) Light of Christ
Moroni 7:24 - Diversity
Moroni 7:33 - Moral Discipline
Moroni 7:41 - Success Strategies
Moroni 7:44 - Faith is a Principle of Power
Moroni 8:8 - Commitment
Moroni 8:25-26 - One Lord, One Faith, One Baptism

Righteous Nephites and wicked Lamanites, as well as everyone else who falls between these two extremes, will be judged by laws to which they were accountable during their lives. Their responsibility before the Judgment Bar, when they are given the opportunity to explain their behavior, will differ, depending upon their singular circumstances. However, the gospel doesn't discriminate, and every Nephite and Lamanite is alike unto God. We all enjoy the Light of Christ that gives us the perspective to see past the limited horizon of our vision, to act upon our promptings, and to do what is right. At the end of the day, each of us has to be individually accountable to God.

Moroni 10:8 - Gifts of The Spirit
Moroni 10:8 - (The) Manifestation of Spirits
Moroni 10:31 - Zion

Moroni 10:31 - (A) Standard of Excellence
Moroni 10:34 - I Have Fought a Good Fight

The Stick of Judah has nourished the Gentiles as manna in the wilderness during their journey to Christ, while the Stick of Joseph is a gift to the Lamanites, as the bread of life to the branch that has grown up beyond the wall.

If you don't find what you are looking for in the Index of Volumes 3 – 7, check out this list of topics with related essay references.

Abstinence – Abstinence in a Permissive World
Accountability – Age of Accountability
Adaptivity – Updates are Ready
Apocrypha – Additional Scripture
Apocrypha – Lost Books of The Bible
Apocrypha – Missing Scripture
Apostolic Church – (The) Church of Jesus Christ in Former Times
Are We Alone in The Universe? – Dancing With the Stars
Attitude- Just Keep Smiling
Authority – Having Been Commissioned of Jesus Christ
Born Again – A Change of Heart
Ceremonies - Types, Rites, Ceremonies, and Symbols
Character – Our Eternal Nature
Charity – Buddy Can You Spare a Dime?
Charity – A Mailbox Marked With an X
Chastity - Abstinence in a Permissive World
Christians – Are Mormons Christians
Christ – What Think Ye of Christ?
Church – Recognizing The Church of Christ
Consequences – The Scope of Our Decisions
Corrections – Writing on Metal Plates Was a Pain
Covenants – Covenant Consciousness
Covenants – The Nature of God and Our Covenants
Cumorah – Were There Two Cumorahs?
Darkness – Light and Darkness
Death – Everyone Wants to Go to Heaven
Dependency – Who is Packing Your Parachute?
Devil – Lucifer
Discipline – Moral Discipline
Doctrine – Teaching Key Doctrine
Evangelicals – Born Again Christians
Evil – Combatting Evil
Excellence – A Standard of Excellence
Faith – Alma's Discourse on Faith
Faith – The Germination of our Faith
Faith – Alma's Discourse on Faith
Feet – The Thrill of Victory / The Agony of DeFeet

Forgiveness – The Door Swings Both Ways
Forgiveness – Father Forgive Them
Freedom of Choice - Agency
Free Will – Agency
Gathering of Israel – The Desert Shall Rejoice
Gifts of The Spirit – Spiritual Gifts
Government – Caesar
Government – Management by The Spirit
Great Apostasy – Apostasy
Heaven – Higher Dimensional Realities
Holy Ghost – Batteries are Not Included
Holy Ghost – God's Tactical Flashlight
Humility – The Dust of The Earth
I Am a Child of God – Spiritual Identity Theft
Immorality - Abstinence in a Permissive World
I Think, Therefore I Am – Cogito, Ergo Sum
Joseph's Technicolor Dream Coat – A Coat of Many Colors
Kindness – Speak Kind Words to Each Other
Knowledge – The Circle of Knowledge
Last Days – The Church in The Last Days
Laughter – Why We Laugh
Light – Walk in The Light
Mercy – Justice and Mercy
Missionary Work – Happiness and Sharing The Gospel
Missionary Work – No Greater Call
Missionary Work – The Number of Disciples Was Multiplied
Missionary Work – Sharing The Gospel
Missionary Work – The Sons of Mosiah
Missionary Work – Strangers in The Land
Music – Worship in Music
Non-members – Strangers in The Land
Omniscience – (The) Q Continuum
One Way – One Lord, One Faith, One Baptism
Opposition – Agency and Opposition
Opposition – Lamanites by The Waters of Sebus
Optimism – Huckleberries and Chokeberries

When the hearts of the Nephites had been bruised by the painful recognition of their sins, it was easier to negotiate the path to repentance. Their hearts were broken and softened and they were responsive to the quiet whisperings of the Spirit. They had become teachable, and their faith had wrought upon them to convict them of their sins. As soon as they had descended into the depths of humility to cast themselves before the altar of Christ, that they might trust upon His Atonement, they were set free from their bondage to sin. His grace blessed them with the unfathomable gift of His unconditional forgiveness.

Peer Pressure – (The) Priests of Baal in Our Lives
Permissiveness – Abstinence in a Permissive World
Perseverance – Just Get Back on The Bike
Personal Responsibility – Work and Personal Responsibility
Plan of Salvation – (The) Hourglass of Life
Plan of Salvation – Life is a Three Act Play
Plates – Writing on Metal Plates Was a Pain
Power – May the 4th Be With You
Preaching the Gospel – Establishing the Word
Preparedness – Spiritual Calisthenics
Priest's Duty – (The) Duty of The Priest
Primitive Church – (The) Church of Jesus Christ in Former Times
Pseudepigrapha – Additional Scripture
Repentance – Before a Wound Can Heal
Repentance – Removing the Barnacles of Life
Responsibility – Work and Personal Responsibility
Restoration – Christ's Church is Restored
Revelation – The Heavens Were Opened
Revelation – Personal Revelation
Revelation – (The) Spirit of Revelation
Revelation – Receiving Revelation
Rites – Types, Rites, Ceremonies, and Symbols
Satan – Lucifer
Scripture Not in The Bible – Additional Scripture

Scriptures – Studying the Scriptures
Speed of Light / Thought – Travel at The Speed of Thought
Spirits – (The) Manifestation of Spirits
Spiritual Fitness – (A) Thirty Day Spiritual Fitness Program
Spiritual Gifts – Gifts of The Spirit
Symbols – Types, Rites, Ceremonies, and Symbols
Technology – Technological Traps
Telestial / Celestial – Jumping Out of Our Skin
Ten Tribes – (The) Lost Ten Tribes
Translation – (A) Whirlwind into Heaven
Truth – Light and Truth
Types – Types, Rites, Ceremonies, and Symbols
Unity – Quorum Sensing
Weakness – Strengths and Weaknesses
Why Things Fall Apart – Entropy in The Physical and Eternal Worlds
Wickedness – Happiness and Wickedness
Wishful Thinking – Too Good to Be True
Word of God – Sharper Than a Two-edged Sword
Work in Progress – Construction Zone: Proceed With Caution
Worship – Worship in Music
Youth – Agency and Youth

When Nephite converts joined the church of Christ, each one was given a gift by the Spirit. These were positive, uplifting, motivational, and enduring. In their fiery crucible that was the learning laboratory of life, it was their spiritual gifts that provided them with repetitive opportunities to vividly role-play being children of God, with the Holy Ghost acting as their dialogue coach. For their life lessons to be helpful, they needed to pre-play and then re-play, and practice over and over again until they got it right, until they could do it with their eyes closed.

Table of Contents

"Scripture consists not in what we read,
but in what we understand."
(St. Hilary).

The worth of principles is validated
by our witness, or our testimony. The Book of
Mormon emphasizes that baptism is the outward
expression of our personal dedication to obedience.
It is the public manifestation of our desire to
have a private covenant relationship with
God. It is the voluntary surrender of
our agency to a higher power,
the subjugation of our
desires to His
will.

Author's Note

Author's Note...1

Introduction

Introduction...3

Hebrew Poetry
In The Book of Mormon

Hebrew Poetry in The Book of Mormo...11

Whenever we undertake a
well-intentioned, comprehensive, and
purposeful examination of The merits of
The Book of Mormon, we are immediately
struck by the realization that our spiritual
awakening will progress only as long as we
are learning. We take solace in the fact that,
although we are admonished 154 times
in the scriptures to be perfect, we are
also encouraged 129 times to
'learn,' and 995 times
to 'begin.'

Synonymous Parallelism

Synonymous Parallelism..21

Antithetical Parallelism

Antithetical Parallelism..39

Synthetic Parallelism

Synthetic Parallelism..55

The Book of Mormon is a wonderful destination, a safe haven, and a sanctuary, where we can all commence our education in the grammar of the gospel. It can be an exclamation point in the process of repentance, and we approach our study with confidence that "at the banquet of consequences, we will be able to bow our heads in reverence, rather than hang them in shame, in the presence of God who will be there." (Marion Hanks).

Climactic Parallelism

Climatic Parallelism..63

Chiasmus

Chiasmus..89

List of Book of Mormon Scriptures that illustrate Hebrew Poetry

List of Book of Mormon Scriptures that illustrate Hebrew Poetry..115

The Book of Mormon is an extraordinary work, validating the supposition that there are rhythms in nature that we can feel only when we are in harmony with eternal principles.

Cognates
In The Book of Mormon

Cognates in The Book of Mormon..129

Observations

Observations..141

Commentary, Compendia, & Observations Index

Commentary, Compendia, & Observations Index..365

Our study of The Book of Mormon rewards us with the illumination of gospel principles that will bathe our minds in a cascade of the celestial diamond dust of inspiration and revelation. We are steadfast in our resolve to repent, and to relinquish our iniquity, as the Spirit reminds us that our pride is nothing less than a frightening after-image of the rebellion of Lucifer when he defiantly stood before the great Council in heaven to promote his own agenda.

Author's Note

These Compendia have taken on a life of their own, expanding into a collection of eight volumes of detailed information about The Book of Mormon that supplement my three volumes of Commentary. In essence, they are a distillation of my feelings that relate to The Book of Mormon. Their content is more visceral that that of the Commentary, and perhaps it more accurately reflects my personal feelings about the monumental themes that run throughout all of scripture. They summarize the more comprehensive body of work in my Commentary and showcase my feelings, in the hope that they might become living documents that not only reflect my present understanding of The Book of Mormon, but also the paradigms that expand with the utilization of new tools of discovery. It's a good bet that there is more to come. As the adage encourages, we need to "Think ourselves empty, read ourselves full, write ourselves clear, pray ourselves hot, and let ourselves go!"

The cataracts that are created by our concessions to sin cloud our vision. Our narrow perspective forces us into making comfortless compromises, leaving the landscapes of our lives as nothing more than empty shells. If we do not take advantage of the therapy of repentance thru the Atonement of Jesus Christ, that is encouraged by every Book of Mormon prophet, the prognosis for success is poor for eyes that have lost the ability to see clearly, and that can no longer make the distinctions between good and evil, between light and darkness, between pleasure and pain, and between virtue and vice.

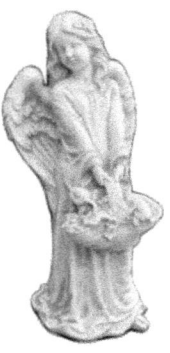

Introduction

Alma taught that, in the absence of their repentance for their sins, and without the benefit of covenants, Adam and Eve would have ultimately been miserable. (See Alma 42:11 & 12:26). To be sure, they would have lived forever, but without the Atonement, it would have been in a state of perpetual alienation from the hearth and home of God.

Cicero wrote: "The first law for the historian is that he shall never dare utter an untruth. The second is that he shall suppress nothing that is true. Moreover, there shall be no suspicion of partiality or of malice in his writing." The accounts in The Book of Mormon written by the prophets Nephi, Jacob, Alma, Mormon, Moroni, and others, and abridged by the prophet-historian Mormon, were true to the mandate given by Cicero. Although, as Washington Irving brooded: "It is the rule that history fades into fable; fact becomes clouded with doubt and controversy; the inscription moulders, and columns, arches, and pyramids are but heaps of sand, and their epitaphs, nothing but characters written in the dust," yet The Book of Mormon stands as a shining example of the divine model.

It "is the witness that testifies to the passing of time. It illuminates reality, vitalizes memory, provides guidance in daily life, and brings us tidings of antiquity." It is the "evidence of time, the light of truth, the life of memory, the directress of life, committed to immortality." (Cicero, "De Oratore," ii, 36). In its pages, "the centuries roll back to the ancient age of gold." (Horace, "Odes," IV, ii, 39).

In one of the beautiful simplicities of the gospel, we are taught that the Plan allows all of us to enjoy the same access to the simplest, and yet most powerful, witness to the truth. In an inarticulate voice softer than the faintest whisper of sweet breath on the cheek, the Holy Ghost gently testifies, or bears witness, of truth. As Moroni 10:5 teaches (in a verse that is often overlooked, in favor of the previous verse): "By the power of the Holy Ghost ye may know the truth of all things."

The Holy Ghost has revealed all that is true, and has illuminated every eternal principle that has guided the minds of men and women since the dawn of history. We constantly benefit from that which He reveals. In the Last Days, when the Spirit is "poured out upon all flesh, and when "young men see visions, and old men dream dreams," (Joel 2:28), it will be the Holy Ghost Who provides the creative drive. The irony is that many will fail to recognize the source of their inspiration. Job did not. He wrote: "For God speaketh once, yea twice, yet man perceiveth it not. In a dream, in a vision of the night, when deep sleep falleth upon men, in slumberings upon the bed; then he openeth the ears of men, and sealeth their instruction." (Job 33:14-16). We cannot help but think of the experience of Joseph Smith in his bedchamber, when we read Job's description of how, at certain times, Heavenly Father chooses to communicate with His children.

All who desire to have a sure personal witnesses must carefully and prayerfully read The Book of Mormon, and then ask in faith if what they have studied is true. They will then receive the testimony of the Holy Ghost to motivate them to seek out the Priesthood and to enter into sacred covenants with God. It will be as it was on the Day of Pentecost, when Peter and others were preaching to a multitude whose hearts and minds were open and receptive to the truth. The words of the Apostles carried the weight of authority, and penetrated the hearts of their listeners to the end that they asked: "Men and brethren, what shall we do? Then Peter said unto them, Repent, and be baptized every one of you in the name of Jesus Christ for the remission of sins, and ye shall receive the gift of the Holy Ghost." (Acts 2:37-38). And on that day, there were about 3,000 souls added to the kingdom of God on earth. (See Commentary Reference to 3 Nephi 15:21-24).

A similar scenario exists today. Since the Restoration of the gospel, there has been a Pentecostal outpouring of the Spirit, and those with a sincere desire to understand the will of God bring the same humble petition to the doorstep of the missionaries: "Now that we have heard your message, have put it to the test of prayerful inquiry, and have received a witness of the Spirit, what shall we do?" The response of the servants of the Lord is unequivocal: "You must exercise saving faith that leads to the waters of baptism and to continuing commitment, dedicated discipleship, selfless service, and sustained spirituality."

Shakespeare wrote: "The past is prologue." ("The Tempest," Act 2, scene 1, 245-254). The phrase was intended to

The Lord said: "I will try the faith of my people." (3 Nephi 26:11). The Book of Mormon itself is a part of that self-administered examination. The Saints are compelled to read and nurture independent testimonies of that volume of scripture. If they do not wholeheartedly embrace the doctrine of Christ contained therein, or do not live up to their covenants, they will be in the power of Satan. The inquisition that accompanied the grand experiment posited by Alma to the poor Zoramites portends an ominous consequence. (See Alma 32). None of us will receive a witness until after the trial of our faith. Only after passing through the refiner's fire will we be as tempered steel in our devotion to the Savior. "I have refined thee," said the Lord, "but not with silver; I have chosen thee in the furnace of affliction." (Isaiah 48:10). "What we obtain too cheap, we esteem too lightly. 'Tis dearness alone that gives everything its value. Heaven knows how to put a proper price on its goods." (Tom Paine).

imply that our past is merely a prologue, or an introduction, to the great adventure upon which we will embark if we follow through on our plans. This original interpretation teaches that what has come before on our journey through life doesn't matter in the grand scheme of things, because a new future lies before us, subject to the choices we will yet make. The human condition does not change much over time, which is one reason why the Lord has revealed The Book of Mormon in the Last Days, so that we might profit from the experiences of the Nephites who are distant from us in time and yet are so like us.

Hugh Nibley observed: "Men fool themselves, when they think for a moment that they can read scripture without ever adding something to the text or omitting something from it." Therein lies the power inherent in its study. We glean insight and understanding every time we investigate the word of God. I have learned to love the scriptures, and I often think of St. Hilary, who wrote: "Scripture consists not in what we read, but in what we understand." In these Compendia, I have consistently tried to anchor to the scriptures the ideas swirling around in my head.

Utilization of commentaries and compendia does not replace personal scripture study. The spiritual awakening that accompanies prayerful efforts to understand the mysteries of God through the study of His word cannot be achieved through another person's interpretation. Perhaps, though, my own perspectives on the eternal themes expressed within The Book of Mormon will be helpful to you as you read and seek your own guidance. It is my hope that you will use these compendia only to assist you in your own personal journey to Christ.

Our challenge is to enlist the aid of the Holy Ghost as we undertake that journey. Many years ago, Dallin Oaks wrote: "Latter-day Saints know that learned or authoritative commentaries (and compendia) can help us with scriptural interpretation, but we maintain that they must be used with caution. (They) are not substitutes for the scriptures any more than a good cookbook is a substitute for food. When I refer to "commentaries," I mean everything that interprets scripture, from the comprehensive book-length commentary to the brief interpretation embodied in a lesson or an article, such as this one."

"One trouble with commentaries," he continued, "is that their authors sometimes focus on only one meaning to the exclusion of others. As a result, commentaries, if not used with great care, may illuminate the author's chosen and correct meaning but close our eyes and restrict our horizons to other possible meanings. Sometimes, those other less obvious meanings can be the ones most valuable and useful to us as we seek to obtain answers to our own questions. This is why the teaching of the Holy Ghost is a better guide to scriptural interpretation than is even the best commentary." ("Ensign," 1/1985).

Harold B. Lee taught: "We are convinced that our members are hungry for the gospel undiluted, with its abundant truths and insights. There are those who have seemed to forget that the most powerful weapons the Lord has given us against all that is evil are His own declarations – the plain and simple doctrines of salvation as found in the scriptures." (Regional Representatives Seminar, 10/1/1970).

Bruce R. McConkie explained that "revelation is necessary because ... each pronouncement in the holy scriptures is so written as to reveal little or much, depending on the spiritual capacity of the student." ("A New Witness for The Articles of Faith," p. 71).

And so, as President Oaks continued, "the scriptures are not the ultimate source of knowledge, but what precedes the ultimate source. The ultimate source comes by revelation. We encourage everyone to make careful study of the scriptures and of prophetic teachings ... and to prayerfully seek personal revelation to know their meaning for themselves ... If we seek and accept revelation and inspiration to enlarge our understanding, we will have the mysteries of God unfolded to us by the power of the Holy Ghost."

Our eternal focus of faith is nurtured when we "discard the poor lenses of our bodies, and are able to peer thru a telescope of truth into the infinite reaches of immortality." (Helen Keller). But if we turn our backs on the invitation to have a relationship with God through The Book of Mormon, and we remain alienated from Him by spiritual death, we will be forced by the Adversary to surrender our fortunes to inclinations that are carnal and sensual.

Bruce R. McConkie also said: "I sometimes think that one of the best kept secrets of the kingdom is that the scriptures open the door to the receipt of revelation." ("Doctrines of The Restoration," p. 243). And President Oaks reaffirmed: "We do not overstate the point when we say that the scriptures can be a Urim and Thummim to assist each of us to receive personal revelation."

President Oaks enlarged upon the perspective of the young prophet: "Joseph was, by his own admission, no writer. He felt imprisoned by what he called the 'total darkness of paper, pen, and ink.'" (Joseph Smith to William W. Phelps, 11/27/1832, B.Y.U. Press, 2002, p. 287). He thus considered it 'an awful responsibility to write in the name of the Lord'. (Joseph Smith Papers, 1:367).

He did not suppose that he could receive the revelations perfectly, nor did the Lord ever set that standard. Joseph and his appointed brethren edited the revelations (see D&C 70:1-4) based on (that) same premise ... namely, that he represented the voice of God as he spoke in what he characterized as his own 'crooked, broken, scattered, and imperfect language'. (Joseph Smith to William W. Phelps, 11/27/1832, quoted in "Making Sense of the Doctrine & Covenants, a Guided Tour Through Modern Revelation," Steven Harper. "Personal Writings of Joseph Smith," p. 186-187).

President Oaks concluded his own epistle by stating a simple truth: "Latter-day Saints know that true doctrine comes by revelation from God, and not by worldly wisdom." (See Moses 5:58). He was in good company, for the Apostle Paul wrote that we are not capable of thinking any thing of ourselves; but we look to God for our wisdom. (See 1 Corinthians 3:5).

I could not agree more heartily with these wise words of counsel. As a matter of fact, every time I proofed my compendium (and I did this many times) I found myself scribbling additional notes in the margins and thinking to myself, "Why didn't I see that before?." That is precisely what I hope will be the experience of everyone who takes the time to read my compendia. I trust the process will motivate you to search the scriptures more carefully and to be instructed by the Spirit, as you do so, that you might be led in directions that will prove to be personally illuminating.

I would expect that my older grandchildren who read this compendium will be impacted in ways that are different from my adult children or my contemporaries. I hope that my observations will touch you differently each time you read them. When I am long-gone, perhaps the considerable thought that went into its production will generate a palpable bond that will span the years separating us. Maybe, the gulf that then divides us will not be as great, and our shared energies will pave the way to an eventual joyous reunion.

Wresting the holy scriptures by suggesting that we are saved by our own works, twists holy writ from its true or proper signification, and perverts it from its correct or its rightful application. Lest we deceive ourselves, let it be known that we all need the clarity of Book of Mormon teachings, if we wish to be saved in the Kingdom of God.

Hebrew Poetry
In The Book of Mormon

The Book of Mormon
encourages us to feast upon
the word of Christ and ponder
the doctrines of the kingdom. We
receive God's strength to endure one
more day in righteousness. Our eyes
remain fixed upon the prize that is
the high calling of Jesus Christ,
and we taste the principles of
eternal life that are taught
with eloquence by its
inspired prophet-
historians.

Nephi explained that latter-
day Israel would need to learn the
things of the Jews (see 2 Nephi 25:5),
to engage in a study of the scriptures that
reveals layers of meaning, until we come to the
point envisioned by the Dead Sea Covenanter,
who wrote: "For mine own part I have reached
the intervision, and through the Spirit
thou hast placed within me, come
to know Thee, my God."
(Eleventh Hymn).

From out of the dust, Nephi wrote of his preferred Hebrew poet: "Wherefore, hearken, O my people, which are of the house of Israel, and give ear unto my words; for because the words of Isaiah are not plain unto you, nevertheless, they are plain unto all those that are filled with the spirit of prophecy." (2 Nephi 25:4).

The poetry of The Book of Mormon may be used as a springboard that catapults us to elevated plateaus of discovery, as we are taught by the Spirit to think as Israelites do, and jump off in the direction of our dreams.

The hallmark of Hebrew poetry is parallelism, which is the echoing of the thought of one line of verse in a second line that is its partner. This is called repetition of thought. Two lines of poetry are said to be parallel if the elements of one line correspond directly to those of the other, in a 1:1 relationship. For example; Lehi" was obedient unto the word of the Lord, wherefore, he did as the Lord commanded him." (1 Nephi 2:3).

There are many variations of parallelism in Hebrew poetry. One is a repetition of the same idea, which is called synonymous parallelism. "Behold, I have dreamed a dream. Or, in other words, I have seen a vision." (Nephi 8:2, with a cognate thrown in, for good measure)! Another illustrates a contrasting idea: "Wherefore, if a man have faith, he must needs have hope; for without faith there cannot be any hope." (Moroni 7:42). A third completes the idea of one line in a second line: "I am filled with charity, which is (God's) everlasting love." (Moroni 8:17).

Antithetical parallelism is a literary device that brings together ideas that contrast each other. Rather than saying the same thing twice, antithetically parallel poetry introduces the concept, and then repeats it in opposite terms. "The things which are pleasing unto the world. I do not write, but the things which are pleasing unto God and unto those who are not of the world." (1 Nephi 6:5).

Synthetic parallelism is a Hebraic literary device that ties together two related thoughts to emphasize behaviors, traits, or similarities, Rather than providing a contrast, or expressing the same idea in different words, as antithetical or synonymous parallelism would do, the second line of synthetic parallelism completes the thought of the first line. "Laban hath a record of the Jews and also a genealogy of my forefathers, and they are engraven upon plates of brass." (1 Nephi 3:3).

Climactic parallel poetry employs words
whose import is repeated in successive lines.
This additional information enlarges upon the
meaning of the passage until the theme that had
been initiated in the first line has been completed
with a dramatic climactic flourish in the last line.
For example: "The Lord knoweth all things from
the beginning; wherefore, he prepareth a way to
accomplish all his works among the children
of men; for behold, he hath all power unto
the fulfilling of all his words."
(1 Nephi 9:6).

Lastly, the device
called a chiasm repeats
line one, but in a reverse order.
If the second line is inverted, that
is to say, if its last element is placed
first, and the first, last, then a chiasm is
created, as in: "I will not put my trust in the
arm of flesh; for I know that cursed is he that
putteth his trust in the arm of flesh. Yea,
cursed is he that putteth his trust in
man, or maketh flesh his arm."
(2 Nephi 4:34).

The repetitive
pattern that is utilized
in Hebrew poetry illustrates
a spaciousness and a dignity that
creates time for the thought to make an
impact on the hearer, and it also provides
an opportunity for the author to offer more
than one perspective. It is unselfconscious,
and remains remarkably free from the
artificialities of language that can
blur the meaning or intent of
its compositions.

Its structure, based as it
is on meaning, survives translation
with remarkably little loss, unlike poetry
that relies on a special vocabulary or a complex
meter. This is particularly significant when we
consider the remarkable fidelity of the translation
into the English language of the ancient records
that were delivered by Moroni into the hands
of the prophet Joseph Smith.

Hebrew poetry has the capacity
to plumb the depths of our own testimonies
by quietly turning our thoughts to our Creator.
It reminds us that our God is in control, and that
by His divine design, those who love and serve Him
in righteousness and who obey His commandments
with exactness, will inherit the mansions that have
been prepared for them. It serenely bears witness of
the divine mission of our Savior. It illuminates
the path we must follow in order to receive the
blessings that are reserved for the faithful. It
teaches us about repentance, atonement,
and forgiveness, about His tender
mercies, and ultimately, about
the Plan of Salvation that
He has crafted for His
children.

As we immerse ourselves
in an earnest study of The Book
of Mormon, our investigation reveals
a polychromatic palette onto which we
may dip the brush of understanding.
With God's gentle guidance, we may
paint broad strokes that capture not
only the compelling reverberations
of its delightful meter, but also
the enchanting detail of its
unexpected beauty.

Book of
Mormon poetry
invites us to immerse
ourselves in the grandeur
of the world; to enjoy a greater
sense of all that's virtuous, lovely,
or of good report, and praiseworthy. It
urges us to heed Nephi's counsel; to press
forward with complete dedication and with
steadfastness, or with confidence, and a firm
determination in Jesus Christ, having a perfect
brightness of hope, or faith, and charity, which
is the love of God, and of men and
women everywhere.

Engaging
The Book of Mormon
is like immersing ourselves
in a temple experience. We look
around ourselves in anticipation,
wondering what we might learn that
is new. Who will our teachers be today,
and how will the principles they desire to
convey be opened to our understanding?
How will the Holy Ghost touch us today?
Will we be inspired with insight, or will
it be intuition, inspiration, or perhaps
the dynamo of revelation that will
distill upon our minds and our
souls as the dews of heaven?

In light of the poetical beauty
of The Book of Mormon, the reality is
that many of those who continue to deny the
divine origin of that text must now admit that
even as they continue to cling to the pretense that
its presentation is apocryphal, at best it remains a
stellar example of an ancient sacred text that makes
a powerful statement regarding its visions, poetry,
parables, and psalms, relating to the worth of
souls in a world where its merits are
nearly universally questioned.

Many forms
of poetry exist in The
Book of Mormon. In fact,
they pervade the text, and they
are often strategically placed in
order to highlight the importance of
particular passages. Even the Bard
of Avon would be impressed by
its grace, beauty, and turn
of phrase.

Synonymous Parallelism

Synonymous parallelism is a literary device that restates the same idea in different words. It utilizes the repetition of one idea in a subsequent line. The first half makes a statement, and the second half says the same thing, with only minor variations. The statements are juxtaposed, with similar syntax.

Old Testament Psalms have been attributed to David, Asaph, and the sons of Korah, (see Psalms 75, 77, & 82, & 1 Chronicles 6:31), who likely belonged to guilds of temple singers. Individual psalms underwent constant adaptation; some were modified for use in the temple, and others were re-worked to fit contemporary circumstances that later only complicated the determination of the date and authorship of the composition.

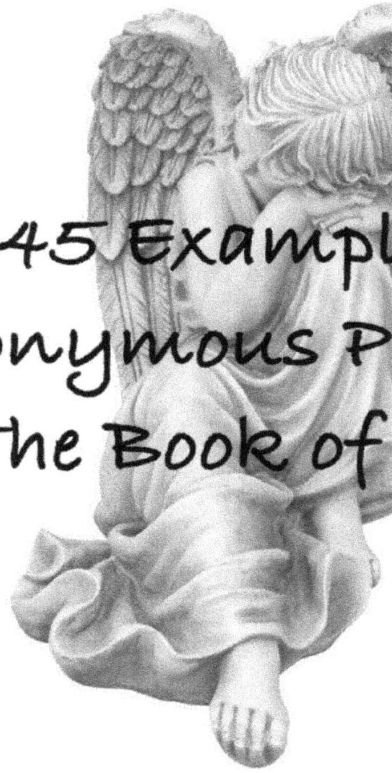

45 Examples of Synonymous Parallelism in The Book of Mormon

"He was
obedient unto
the word of the Lord,
wherefore, he did as the
Lord commanded him."
(1 Nephi 2:3).

"They did murmur in many things
against their father, because he was a
visionary man, and had led them out of
the land of Jerusalem, to leave the land of
their inheritance, and their gold, and their
silver, and their precious things, to perish
in the wilderness. And this they said
he had done because of the foolish
imaginations of his heart."
(1 Nephi 2:11).

"He said that
these plates of brass should
not perish; neither should they be
dimmed any more by time."
(1 Nephi 5:19).

"Behold, I have dreamed a
dream; or, in other words,
I have seen a vision."
(1 Nephi 8:2).

"Upon the
other plates should be engraven
an account of the reign of the kings,
and the wars and contentions of my people;
wherefore, these plates are for the more part of
the ministry; and the other plates are for
the more part of the reign of the kings
and the wars and contentions of
my people." (1 Nephi 9:4).

"I spake
unto him as a man
speaketh; for I beheld that
he was in the form of a man;
yet nevertheless, I knew that it
was the Spirit of the Lord; and
he spake unto me as a man
speaketh with another."
(1 Nephi 11:11).

"Behold the Lamb of
God, yea, even the Son
of the Eternal Father!"
(1 Nephi 11:21).

"I looked and
beheld the Lamb of God, that
he was taken by the people; yea,
the Son of the everlasting God
was judged of the world."
(1 Nephi 11:32).

"It came to pass that
I beheld multitudes gathered
together to battle, one against the
other; and I beheld wars, and rumors
of wars, and great slaughters with
the sword among my people."
(1 Nephi 12:2).

"Behold,
the Lord hath created the
earth that it should be inhabited;
and he hath created his children
that they should possess it."
(1 Nephi 17:36).

"He
ruleth
high in the
heavens, for it is
his throne, and this
earth is his footstool."
(1 Nephi 17:39).

"Behold, my soul is rent with
anguish because of you, and my
heart is pained; I fear lest ye shall be
cast off forever. Behold, I am full of
the Spirit of God, insomuch that
my frame has no strength."
(1 Nephi 17:47).

"The Lord said unto me: Stretch forth thine hand again unto thy brethren, and they shall not wither before thee, but I will shock them, saith the Lord, and this will I do, that they may know that I am the Lord their God. And it came to pass, that I stretched forth my hand unto my brethren, and they did not wither before me; but the Lord did shake them, even according to the word which he had spoken." (1 Nephi 17:53-54).

"We did begin to till the earth, and we began to plant seeds; yea, we did put all our seeds into the earth." (1 Nephi 18:24).

"Behold, I have refined thee; I have chosen thee in the furnace of affliction." (1 Nephi 20:10).

"In the
shadow of his hand
hath he hid me, and made
me a polished shaft; in his
quiver hath he hid me."
(1 Nephi 21:2).

"Say to
the prisoners:
Go forth; to them
that sit in darkness:
Show yourselves."
(1 Nephi 21:9).

"Blessed art thou,
and thy seed for thou shalt
inherit the land like unto thy brother
Nephi. And thy seed shall be numbered
with his seed; and thou shalt be even like
unto thy brother, and thy seed like
unto his seed; and thou shalt be
blessed in all thy days."
(2 Nephi 4:11).

"I clothe the heavens
with blackness, and I make
sackcloth their covering."
(2 Nephi 7:3).

"Pray unto him
continually by day
and give thanks unto his
holy name by night."
(2 Nephi 9:52).

"Praise the Lord; call upon
his name; declare his doings
among the people; make mention
that his name is exalted."
(2 Nephi 22:4).

"The Jews shall be scattered among all nations; yea, and also, Babylon shall be destroyed; wherefore, the Jews shall be scattered by other nations."
(2 Nephi 25:15).

"It shall come to pass in that day that the churches which are built up, and not unto the Lord, when the one shall say unto the other: Behold, I, I am the Lord's; and the others shall say: I, I am the Lord's; and thus shall every one say that hath built up churches, and not unto the Lord."
(2 Nephi 28:3).

"The things
of all nations shall be
made known; yea, all things
shall be made known unto
the children of men."
(2 Nephi 30:16).

"And we also had many
revelations, and the spirit of much
prophecy; wherefore, we knew of
Christ and his kingdom,
which should come."
(Jacob 1:6).

"As many as would
hearken unto the voice of the
Lord should also depart out of the land
with him, in the wilderness. And it came to
pass that he did according as the Lord had
commanded him. And they departed out
of the land into the wilderness, as
many as would hearken unto
the voice of the Lord."
(Omni 1:12-13).

"And I do this for a wise purpose; for thus it whispereth (to) me, according to the workings of the Spirit of the Lord which is in me. And now, I do not know all things; but the Lord knoweth all things which are to come; wherefore, he worketh in me to do according to his will."
(Words of Mormon 1:7).

"There were a great number, even so many that they did not number them; for they had multiplied exceedingly and waxed great in the land."
(Mosiah 2:2).

"This mortal shall put on immortality, and this corruption shall put on incorruption."
(Mosiah 16:10).

"They
find a land which had
been peopled; yea, a land which
was covered with dry bones; yea, a
land which had been peopled and
which had been destroyed."
(Mosiah 21:26).

"They
pitched their tents, and
began to till the ground, and
began to build buildings; yea,
they were industrious, and
did labor exceedingly."
(Mosiah 23:5).

"The Lord seeth fit to chasten
his people; yea, he trieth their
patience and their faith."
(Mosiah 23:21).

"Those whom he had sent out
to watch the camp of the Amlicites
were called Zeram, and Amnor, and
Manti, and Limher; these were they who
went out with their men to watch
the camp of the Amlicites."
(Alma 2:22).

"He
began to
teach the people
in the land of Melek
according to the holy order
of God, by which he had been
called; and he began to teach
the people throughout all
the land of Melek."
(Alma 8:4).

"We will give up
the land of Jershon, which is on
the east by the sea, which joins the land
Bountiful, which is on the south of the land
Bountiful; and this land Jershon is the
land which we will give unto our
brethren for an inheritance."
(Alma 27:22).

"This life
is the time for men
to prepare to meet God;
yea, behold the day of this
life is the day for men to
perform their labors."
(Alma 34:32).

"The soul shall be restored to
the body, and the body to the soul;
yea, and every limb and joint shall
be restored to its body; yea, even a hair
of the head shall not be lost; but all
things shall be restored to their
proper and perfect frame."
(Alma 40:23).

"Behold, they do not desire that
the Lord their God, who hath created
them, should rule and reign over them;
notwithstanding his great goodness
and his mercy towards them, they
do set at naught his counsels,
and they will not that he
should be their guide."
(Helaman 12:6).

"My
people shall know
my name; yea, in that
day they shall know that I
am he that doth speak."
(3 Nephi 20:39).

"It is by
the wicked that the
wicked are punished; f
or it is the wicked that stir
up the hearts of the children
of men unto bloodshed."
(Mormon 4:5).

"God is the same
yesterday, today, and
forever, and in him there
is no variableness neither
shadow of changing."
(Mormon 9:9).

"Thus,
didst thou manifest
thyself unto thy disciples;
for after they had faith, and
did speak in thy name, thou
didst show thyself unto
them in great power."
(Ether 12:31).

"Every man did
cleave unto that which was his
own, with his hands, and would
not borrow, neither would he lend;
and every man kept the hilt of his
sword in his right hand."
(Ether 14:2).

"That which is of God inviteth
and enticeth to do good continually;
wherefore, everything which inviteth
and enticeth to do good, and to
love God, and to serve him,
is inspired of God."
(Moroni 7:13).

Antithetical Parallelism

Antithetical
parallelism describes a literary
device that brings together ideas that
contrast each other. Rather than saying
the same thing twice, antithetically
parallel poetry will introduce a
concept, and then repeat it
in opposite terms.

Latter-day readers
who understand what
type of literary device has
been employed by the author
of scripture are able to better
understand the intent of the
messages that are being
conveyed.

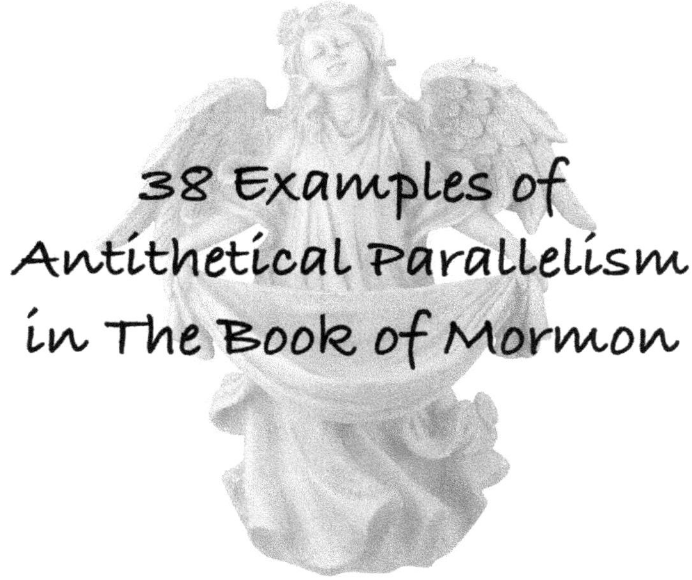

38 Examples of Antithetical Parallelism in The Book of Mormon

"Inasmuch
as ye shall keep
my commandments, ye
shall prosper, and shall be
led to a land of promise, yea,
even a land which I have prepared
for you; yea, a land which is choice
above all other lands. And inasmuch
as thy brethren shall rebel against
thee, they shall be cut off from
the presence of the Lord."
(1 Nephi 2:20-21).

"The things which are
pleasing unto the world I do not write,
but the things which are pleasing unto God and
unto those who are not of the world." (1 Nephi 6:5).

"I beheld
that the power of
God was with them,
and also, that the wrath
of God was upon all those
that were gathered together
against them to battle."
(1 Nephi 13:18).

"I said unto them:
Have ye inquired of
the Lord? And they said
unto me: We have not; for
the Lord maketh no such
thing known unto us."
(1 Nephi 15:8-9).

"Notwithstanding we
had suffered many afflictions
and much difficulty, yea, even so
much that we cannot write them all,
we were exceedingly rejoiced when
we came to the seashore; and we
called the place Bountiful."
(1 Nephi 17:6).

"He raiseth up a righteous
nation, and destroyeth the
nations of the wicked."
(1 Nephi 17:37).

"And he leadeth away the righteous into precious lands, and the wicked he destroyeth, and curseth the land unto them for their sakes."
(1 Nephi 17:38).

"Ye are swift to do iniquity but slow to remember the Lord your God."
(1 Nephi 17:45).

"The things which some men esteem to be of great worth, both to the body and soul, others set at naught and trample under their feet."
(1 Nephi 19:7).

"If iniquity shall
abound, cursed shall be
the land for their sakes, but
unto the righteous it shall
be blessed forever."
(2 Nephi 1:7).

"Inasmuch as ye shall
keep my commandments,
ye shall prosper in the land; but
inasmuch as ye will not keep my
commandments, ye shall be cut
off from my presence."
(2 Nephi 1:20).

"Now, my sons, I would
that ye should look to the great
Mediator, and hearken unto his great
commandments; and be faithful unto his
words, and choose eternal life, according to the
will of his Holy Spirit; And not choose eternal
death, according to the will of the flesh and the
evil which is therein, which giveth the spirit
of the devil power to captivate, to bring you
down to hell, that he may reign over
you in his own kingdom."
(2 Nephi 2:28-29).

"When I
desire to rejoice,
my heart groaneth
because of my sins."
(2 Nephi 4:19).

"They
who are righteous
shall be righteous still,
and they who are filthy
shall be filthy still."
(2 Nephi 9:16).

"He commandeth all men that
they must repent and be baptized
in his name, having perfect faith in the
Holy One of Israel, or they cannot be saved in
the kingdom of God. And if they will not repent
and believe in his name, and be baptized in his
name, and endure to the end, they must be
damned; for the Lord God, the Holy
One of Israel, has spoken it."
(2 Nephi 9:23-24).

"To be carnally-minded is death, and to be spiritually-minded is life eternal."
(2 Nephi 9:39).

"It shall come to pass, instead of sweet smell, there shall be stink; and instead of a girdle, a rent; and instead of well-set hair, baldness, and instead of a stomacher, a girdling of sackcloth; burning instead of beauty."
(2 Nephi 13:24).

"If ye would hearken unto the spirit which teacheth a man to pray, ye would know that ye must pray; for the evil spirit teacheth not a man to pray, but teacheth him that he must not pray."
(2 Nephi 33:8).

"I shall call them Lamanites that seek to destroy the people of Nephi, and those who are friendly to Nephi I shall call Nephites."
(Jacob 1:14).

"How
blessed are
they who have
labored diligently
in his vineyard; and
how cursed are they who
shall be cast out into
their own place!"
(Jacob 6:3).

"We had
many seasons
of peace; and we had
many seasons of serious
war and bloodshed."
(Omni 1:3).

"There is nothing which is good save it comes from the Lord; and that which is evil cometh from the devil."
(Omni 1:25).

"I give not because I have not, but if I had, I would give."
(Mosiah 4:24).

"My soul hath been redeemed from the gall of bitterness and bonds of iniquity. I was in the darkest abyss; but now I behold the marvelous light of God. My soul was racked with eternal torment; but I am snatched, and my soul is pained no more."
(Mosiah 27:29).

"Whatsoever is
good cometh from
God, and whatsoever is
evil cometh from the devil."
(Alma 5:40).

"If
they have
been righteous,
they shall reap the
power and deliverance
of Jesus Christ; and if they
have been evil, they shall reap
the damnation of their souls,
according to the power and
captivation of the devil."
(Alma 9:28).

"If ye will
repent, ye shall be
saved, and if ye will not
repent, ye shall be cast
off at the last day."
(Alma 22:6).

"Yea, I say unto
you, my son, that there could be
nothing so exquisite and so bitter as
were my pains. Yea, and again I
say unto you, my son, that on
the other hand, there can be
nothing so exquisite and
sweet as was my joy."
(Alma 36:21).

"Enter ye in at the
strait gate; for strait is the
gate, and narrow is the way that
leads to life, and few there be that
find it; but wide is the gate, and
broad the way which leads to
death, and many there be
that travel therein."
(3 Nephi 27:33).

"And I did endeavor to preach
unto this people, but my mouth was
shut, and I was forbidden that I
should preach unto them."
(Mormon 1:16).

"They did not
come unto Jesus with
broken hearts and contrite
spirits, but they did curse
God, and wish to die."
(Mormon 2:14).

"The strength of the Lord
was not with us; yea, we were
left to ourselves, that the Spirit
of the Lord did not abide in us;
therefore, we had become weak
like unto our brethren."
(Mormon 2:26).

"He that believeth
and is baptized shall be
saved; but he that believeth
not shall be damned."
(Ether 4:18).

"Thou hast made our words powerful and great, even that we cannot write them; wherefore, when we write, we behold our weakness, and stumble because of the placing of our words."
(Ether 12:25).

"A bitter fountain cannot bring forth good water; neither can a good fountain bring forth bitter water; wherefore, a man being a servant of the devil cannot follow Christ; and if he follow Christ he cannot be a servant of the devil."
(Moroni 7:11).

"For behold, the Spirit
of Christ is given to every man, that he may know
good from evil; wherefore, I show unto you the way to judge;
for every thing which inviteth to do good, and to persuade to
believe in Christ, is sent forth by the power and gift of Christ;
wherefore ye may know with a perfect knowledge it is of God.
But whatsoever thing persuadeth men to do evil, and believe
not in Christ, and deny him, and serve not God, then ye
may know with a perfect knowledge it is of the devil;
for after this manner doth the devil work, for he
persuadeth no man to do good, no, not one;
neither do his angels; neither do they
who subject themselves unto him."
(Moroni 7:16-17).

"Wherefore,
if a man have faith, he must
needs have hope; for without faith
there cannot be any hope."
(Moroni 7:42).

Synthetic Parallelism

Synthetic
parallelism is a
device that very adroitly
links together related thoughts
to emphasize behaviors, traits, or
similarities. Rather than providing a
contrast by expressing the same idea in
different words, as would antithetical or
synonymous parallelism, it becomes the
second line of synthetic parallelism that
completes the thought process that was
initiated in the first line.

Typically, synthetic parallelism is
composed of two or more elements, with
those that follow the first adding new or
instructive explanation. A relationship is
often established between actions, with
subsequent phrases describing the
consequences of the first
phrase.

Synthetic parallelism
is characteristically composed of
just two lines, neither of which are
synonymous or antithetical. Rather,
in this poetic verse, line two provides
explanation and adds something
new or instructive by building
upon the first line.

Each of the related elements that
are representative of synthetic parallelism
builds upon the previous elements, creating a
synthesis that is neither synonymous nor
antithetical. Instead, the first line simply
states an event, and the second states
the conclusion. Together, the parts
may convey cause and effect,
or the second line may
simply clarify the
first.

Clearly, synthetic Hebraic scripture is a broad category, but basically, when its poetical structure is neither synonymous, antithetical, nor climactic, nor does it follow a chiastic pattern, it could be considered to be synthetic.

Not to confuse the issue, but synthetic parallel poetry may also embrace the concept that one thing is better than another.

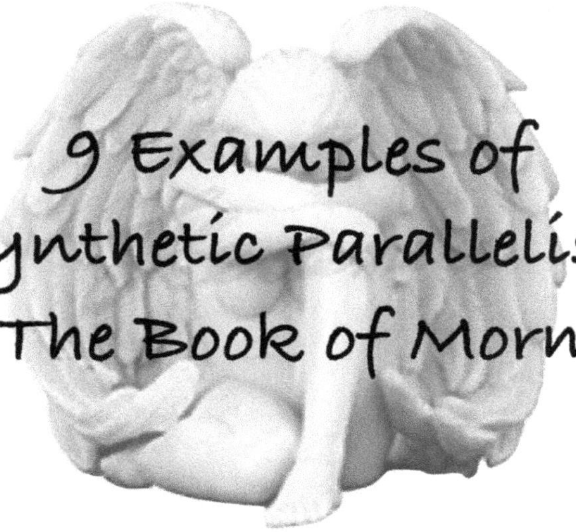

9 Examples of Synthetic Parallelism in The Book of Mormon

"Adam fell, that men might
be, and men are, that they might
have joy. And the Messiah cometh
in the fulness of time, that He
might redeem the children
of men from the fall."
(2 Nephi 2:25).

"His name shall be called after me; and it
shall be after the name of his father. And he
shall be like unto me; for the thing, which
the Lord shall bring forth by his hand,
by the power of the Lord shall bring
my people unto salvation."
(2 Nephi 3:15).

"God will give liberally to him that
asketh. Yea, my God will give me, if I
ask not amiss; therefore I will lift up my
voice unto thee; yea, I will cry unto thee,
my God, the rock of my righteousness.
Behold, my voice shall forever ascend
up unto thee, my rock and mine
everlasting God. Amen."
(2 Nephi 4:35).

"Wo unto the deaf that will
not hear; for they shall perish. Wo
unto the blind that will not see; for they
shall perish also. Wo unto the uncircumcised
of heart, for a knowledge of their iniquities shall
smite them at the last day. Wo unto the liar, for he
shall be thrust down to hell. Wo unto the murderer,
who deliberately killeth, for he shall die. Wo unto
them who commit whoredoms, for they shall
be thrust down to hell. Yea, wo unto those
that worship idols, for the devil of all
devils delighteth in them."
(2 Nephi 9:31-37).

"And now I, Nephi, cannot write all
the things which were taught among my
people; neither am I mighty in writing, like
unto speaking; for when a man speaketh
by the power of the Holy Ghost the power
of the Holy Ghost carrieth it unto the
hearts of the children of men."
(2 Nephi 33:1).

"Hearken, O ye house of Israel,
and hear the words of me,
a prophet of the Lord.
(Jacob 5:2).

"The Lord seeth fit to chasten his people; yea, he trieth their patience and their faith."
(Mosiah 23:21).

"O how great is the nothingness of the children of men; yea, even they are less than the dust of the earth."
(Helaman 12:7).

"And I am filled with charity, which is everlasting love; wherefore, all children are alike unto me; wherefore, I love little children with a perfect love; and they are all alike and partakers of salvation."
(Moroni 8:17).

Climactic Parallelism

Climactic parallel
poetry utilizes words that are
successively repeated, with additional
information that enlarges the meaning,
until the climactic theme that had been
initiated in the first line is stated. The
B line echoes part of the A line, but it
then adds phrasing that develops
the meaning and completes
the thought.

The thought
is developed through
repetition, and it builds to
a climax with the additional
material that's been presented as
the verse reaches its conclusion.
In other words, the second unit
partially balances the first,
but also adds a summary
thought or completes
the series.

Climactic parallelism is
a poetic feature in both the Bible and The Book
of Mormon that occurs when the second unit of a series
balances the first, while also adding a summary thought
completing the process. It occurs when the same word or words
are found in successive sentences, resulting in a continuation
of the thought process from one sentence to the next. This builds
power, while connecting the lines into an inseparable body,
demonstrating a progression of ideas through the
recurrence of identical or similar words,
progressing to a climax.

While climactic parallelism
may be found in ancient Hebraic literature, it
is not as distinctive as some of the other forms of
parallel poetry, because its structure is more loosely
defined. Nevertheless, the fact that it is present in
The Book of Mormon provides evidence of the
literary sophistication of the text, which
is consistent with the claim of
its Hebraic origins.

Hebrew poetry is found throughout The Book of Mormon; you just need to have the ear to recognize it. Readers are only now becoming acquainted with the many forms of parallelism that pervade the text. These are frequently strategically placed to highlight the importance of specific passages.

It really should come as no surprise "that the literary features of The Book of Mormon that Christian ministers have objected to the most are the ones that are pure Hebrew traits. They were woefully ignorant of early Hebrew literary standards, or maliciously intent upon prejudicing the minds of readers when they've raised their voices strongest against the sections that have turned out to be literal translations from the Hebrew."
(Cecil McGavin, 1942).

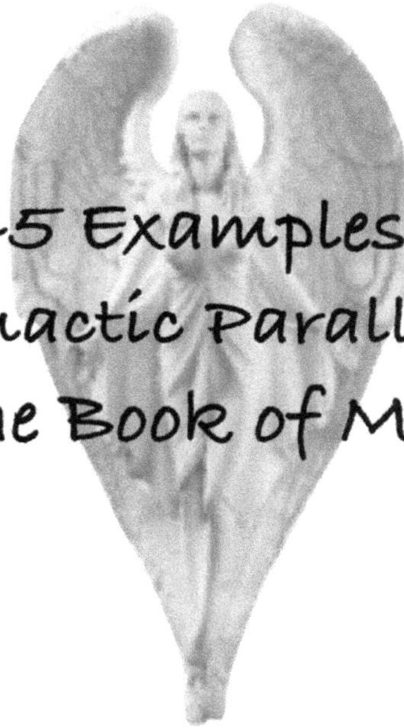

45 Examples of Climactic Parallelism in The Book of Mormon

"He came down by
the borders near the shore of
the Red Sea; and he traveled in the
wilderness in the borders which are
nearer the Red Sea; and he did
travel in the wilderness
with his family."
(1 Nephi 2:5).

"I will go and
do the things which the Lord
hath commanded, for I know that
the Lord giveth no commandments
unto the children of men, save he shall
prepare a way for them that they may
accomplish the thing which he
commandeth them."
(1 Nephi 3:7).

"How is it that
ye have forgotten that ye have seen
an angel of the Lord? Yea, and how is it
that ye have forgotten what great things the
Lord hath done for us, in delivering us out of
the hands of Laban, and also that we should
obtain the record? Yea, and how is it that ye
have forgotten that the Lord is able to do
all things according to his will, for the
children of men, if it so be that they
exercise faith in him? Wherefore,
let us be faithful to him."
(1 Nephi 7:10-12).

"He spake
unto them concerning the Jews, that
after they should be destroyed, even that
great city Jerusalem, and many be carried
away captive into Babylon, according to
the own due time of the Lord, they should
return again, yea, even be brought back
out of captivity; and after they should
be brought back out of captivity they
should possess again the land
of their inheritance." (1
Nephi 10:2-3).

"Wherefore, if they should die in their wickedness they must be cast off also, as to the things which are spiritual, which are pertaining to righteousness; wherefore, they must be brought to stand before God, to be judged of their works; and if their works have been filthiness they must needs be filthy; and if they be filthy it must needs be that they cannot dwell in the kingdom of God; if so, the kingdom of God must be filthy also." (1 Nephi 15:33).

"And it came to pass that according to his word he did destroy them; and according to his word he did lead them; and according to his word he did do all things for them; and there was not any thing done save it were by his word." (1 Nephi 17:31).

"I, Nephi, did not
work the timbers after the
manner which was learned by
men, neither did I build the ship
after the manner of men; but I did
build it after the manner which
the Lord had shown unto me;
wherefore, it was not after
the manner of men."
(1 Nephi 18:2).

"We did begin to till the earth,
and we began to plant seeds; yea, we
did put all our seeds into the earth, which
we had brought from the land of Jerusalem.
And it came to pass that they did grow
exceedingly; wherefore, we were
blessed in abundance."
(1 Nephi 18:22).

"Then will he remember the covenants which he made to their fathers. Yea, then will he remember the isles of the sea; yea, and all the people who are of the house of Israel, will I gather in, saith the Lord, according to the words of the prophet Zenos, from the four quarters of the earth. Yea, and all the earth shall see the salvation of the Lord, saith the prophet; every nation, kindred, tongue and people shall be blessed."
(1 Nephi 19:15-17).

"Hear ye the words of the prophet, ye who are a remnant of the house of Israel, a branch who have been broken off; hear ye the words of the prophet, which were written unto all the house of Israel, and liken them unto yourselves, that ye may have hope as well as your brethren from whom ye have been broken off; for after this manner has the prophet written." (1 Nephi 19:24).

"We have obtained
a land of promise, a land
which is choice above all other
lands; a land which the Lord God
hath covenanted with me should be a
land for the inheritance of my seed. Yea,
the Lord hath covenanted this land unto
me, and to my children forever."
(2 Nephi 1:5).

"O that ye
would awake; awake
from a deep sleep, yea, even
from the sleep of hell, and shake
off the awful chains by which ye
are bound, which are the chains which
bind the children of men, that they are
carried away captive down to the eternal
gulf of misery and woe. Awake! and
arise from the dust, and hear the
words of a trembling parent."
(2 Nephi 1:13-14).

"Men are instructed sufficiently that they know good from evil. And the law is given unto men. And by the law no flesh is justified; or by the law men are cut off. Yea, by the temporal law they were cut off; and also, by the spiritual law they perish from that which is good, and become miserable forever. Wherefore, redemption cometh in and through the Holy Messiah."
(2 Nephi 2:5-6).

"The wolf also shall dwell with the lamb, and the leopard shall lie down with the kid, and the calf and the young lion and fatling together; and a little child shall lead them. And the cow and the bear shall feed; their young ones shall lie down together; and the lion shall eat straw like the ox. And the sucking child shall play on the hole of the asp, and the weaned child shall put forth his hand on the cockatrice's den. They shall not hurt nor destroy in all my holy mountain, for the earth shall be full of the knowledge of the Lord, as the waters cover the sea."
(2 Nephi 2:6-9).

"If ye shall say there is no law, ye shall also say there is no sin. If ye shall say there is no sin, ye shall also say there is no righteousness. And if there be no righteousness there be no happiness. And if there be no righteousness nor happiness there be no punishment nor misery. And if these things are not there is no God. And if there is no God we are not, neither the earth; for there could have been no creation of things, neither to act nor to be acted upon; wherefore, all things must have vanished away."
(2 Nephi 2:13).

"We did take our tents and whatsoever things were possible for us, and did journey in the wilderness for the space of many days. And after we had journeyed for the space of many days, we did pitch our tents."
(2 Nephi 5:7).

"The Lord God said unto me: They shall be a scourge unto thy seed, to stir them up in remembrance of me; and inasmuch as they will not remember me, and hearken unto my words, they shall scourge them, even unto destruction."
(2 Nephi 5:25).

"As death hath passed upon all men to fulfil the merciful plan of the great Creator, there must needs be a power of resurrection, and the resurrection must needs come unto man by reason of the fall; and the fall came by reason of transgression; and because man became fallen they were cut off from the presence of the Lord. Wherefore, it must needs be an infinite atonement."
(2 Nephi 9:6-7).

"And this
death of which I have
spoken, which is the spiritual
death, shall deliver up its dead;
which spiritual death is hell; wherefore,
death and hell must deliver up their dead,
and hell must deliver up its captive spirits,
and the grave must deliver up its captive
bodies, and the bodies and the spirits
of men will be restored one to the
other; and it is by the power
of the resurrection of the
Holy One of Israel."
(2 Nephi 9:12).

"He has given a law; and
where there is no law given
there is no punishment; and
where there is no punishment
there is no condemnation; and
where there is no condemnation
the mercies of the Holy One of
Israel have claim upon them,
because of the atonement;
for they are delivered by
the power of him." (2
Nephi 9:25).

"The stars
of heaven and
the constellations
thereof shall not give
their light; the sun shall
be darkened in his going
forth, and the moon shall
not cause her light to
shine." (2 Nephi
23:10).

"I shall
speak unto the
Jews and they shall
write it; and I shall also
speak unto the Nephites and
they shall write it; and I shall
also speak unto the other tribes of
the house of Israel, which I have led
away, and they shall write it; and
I shall also speak unto all nations
of the earth and they shall write
it." (2 Nephi 29:12).

"Seek
not to counsel
the Lord, but to take
counsel from his hand.
For behold, ye yourselves
know that he counseleth in
wisdom, and in justice,
and in great mercy,
over all his works."
(Jacob 4:10).

"My soul hungered,
and I kneeled down before
my Maker, and I cried unto him
in mighty prayer and supplication
for mine own soul; and all the day long
did I cry unto him; yea, and when the night
came I did still raise my voice high that it
reached the heavens. And there came a
voice unto me, saying: Enos, thy
sins are forgiven thee, and
thou shalt be blessed."
(Enos 1:4-5).

"They have
taught their children that they
should hate them, and that they should
murder them, and that they should rob and
plunder them, and do all they could to
destroy them; therefore, they have
an eternal hatred towards
the children of Nephi."
(Mosiah 10:17).

"Having
gone according
to their own carnal
wills and desires; having
never called upon the Lord while
the arms of mercy were extended
towards them; for the arms of mercy
were extended towards them, and they
would not; they being warned of their
iniquities and yet they would not
depart from them; and they were
commanded to repent and yet
they would not repent."
(Mosiah 16:12).

"If thou hast not found me to be an unprofitable servant, or if thou hast hitherto listened to my words in any degree, and they have been of service to thee, even so I desire that thou wouldst listen to my words at this time, and I will be thy servant and deliver this people out of bondage."
(Mosiah 22:4).

"Ye workers of iniquity; ye that are puffed up in the vain things of the world, ye that have professed to have known the ways of righteousness, nevertheless, have gone astray, as sheep having no shepherd, notwithstanding a shepherd hath called after you and is still calling after you, but ye will not hearken unto his voice!" (Alma 5:37).

"In the eleventh year of the
reign of the judges over the people
of Nephi, on the fifth day of the second
month, there having been much peace in the
land of Zarahemla, there having been (neither)
wars nor contentions for a certain number
of years, even until the fifth day of the
second month in the eleventh year,
there was a cry of war heard
throughout the land."
(Alma 16:1).

"As the preaching of
the word had a great tendency to
lead the people to do that which was just;
yea, it had had more powerful effect upon
the minds of the people than the sword, or
anything else, which had happened unto
them, therefore, Alma thought it was
expedient that they should try the
virtue of the word of God."
(Alma 31:5).

"It is well that ye are cast out of your synagogues, that ye may be humble, and that ye may learn wisdom; for it is necessary that ye should learn wisdom; for it is because that ye are cast out, that ye are despised of your brethren because of your exceeding poverty, that ye are brought to a lowliness of heart, for ye are necessarily brought to be humble."
(Alma 32:12).

"Because ye are compelled to be humble blessed are ye; for a man sometimes, if he is compelled to be humble, seeketh repentance; and now surely, whosoever repenteth shall find mercy; and he that findeth mercy and endureth to the end, the same shall be saved."
(Alma 32:13).

"Because of this great
thing which my people, the Nephites, had done,
they began to boast in their own strength, and (they)
began to swear before the heavens that they would avenge
themselves of the blood of their brethren who had been
slain by their enemies. And they did swear by
the heavens, and also by the throne of God,
that they would go up to battle against
their enemies, and would cut them
off from the face of the land."
(Mormon 3:9-10).

"I had led them, notwithstanding their
wickedness, I had led them many times to battle, and
had loved them, according to the love of God which
was in me, with all my heart; and my soul had
been poured out in prayer unto my God all
the day long for them; nevertheless, it
was without faith, because of the
hardness of their hearts."
(Mormon 3:12).

"I am the same who hideth
up this record unto the Lord; the
plates thereof are of no worth, because of
the commandment of the Lord. For he truly
saith that no one shall have them to get gain;
but the record thereof is of great worth;
and whoso shall bring it to light,
him will the Lord bless."
(Mormon 8:14).

"If men come unto
me I will show unto them
their weakness. I give unto men
weakness that they may be humble;
and my grace is sufficient for all men
that humble themselves before me; for
if they humble themselves before me,
and have faith in me, then will I
make weak things become
strong unto them."
(Ether 12:27).

"Thou hast
prepared a house for man,
yea, even among the mansions of
thy Father, in which man might have
a more excellent hope; wherefore man
must hope, or he cannot receive an
inheritance in the place which
thou hast prepared."
(Ether 12:32).

"There
began to be a great
curse upon all the land
because of the iniquity of
the people, in which, if a man
should lay his tool or his sword
upon his shelf, or upon the place
whither he would keep it, behold,
upon the morrow he could not
find it, so great was the
curse upon the land."
(Ether 14:1).

"God will show unto you, with power and great glory at the last day, that they are true, and if they are true has the day of miracles ceased? Or have angels ceased to appear unto the children of men? Or has he withheld the power of the Holy Ghost from them? Or will he, so long as time shall last, or the earth shall stand, or there shall be one man upon the face thereof to be saved?"
(Moroni 7:35-36).

"None is acceptable before God, save the meek and lowly in heart; and if a man be meek and lowly in heart, and confess by the power of the Holy Ghost that Jesus is the Christ, he must needs have charity; for if he have not charity he is nothing; wherefore he must needs have charity ..... Wherefore, my beloved brethren, if ye have not charity, ye are nothing, for charity never faileth. Wherefore, cleave unto charity, which is the greatest of all."
(Moroni 7:44 & 46).

"Yea, come unto Christ, and be perfected in him, and deny yourselves of all ungodliness; and if ye shall deny yourselves of all ungodliness, and love God with all your might, mind and strength, then is his grace sufficient for you, that by his grace ye may be perfect in Christ; and if by the grace of God ye are perfect in Christ, ye can in nowise deny the power of God." (Moroni 10:32).

repentance is baptism; and baptism cometh by faith unto the fulfilling the commandments; and the fulfilling the commandments bringeth remission of sins; and the remission of sins bringeth meekness, and lowliness of heart; and because of meekness and lowliness of heart cometh the visitation of the Holy Ghost, which Comforter filleth with hope and perfect love, which love endureth by diligence unto prayer, until the end shall come, when all the saints shall dwell with God." (Moroni 8:26-26).

Chiasmus

Chiasmus describes the
intentional reversal of the words
in a poetical repetition. The idea of
line one is repeated in reverse order.
If the second line of parallel verse
is inverted, that is to say, if its
last element is placed first,
and the first, last, then
a chiasm is created.

Virtually since its publication,
enthusiastic supporters of the premise
that The Book of Mormon was of divine
origin have asserted that it reads like a Hebrew
text, while its detractors have taken a vigorously
opposing view. The one thing they've had in common
was that neither were citing very many examples. The
discovery of chiasmus within the book, which bears the
distinct stamp of an ancient Hebraic literary form,
has weighted the scale in favor of its supporters,
and has put its detractors on the defensive,
almost to the point, one might say, that
they are up against the ropes.

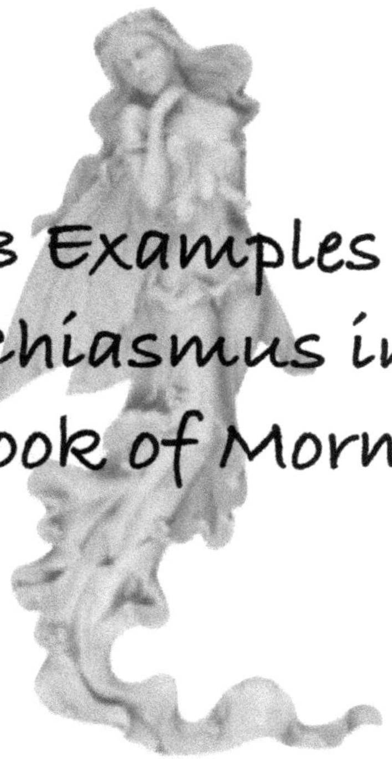

53 Examples of Chiasmus in The Book of Mormon

"I, Nephi, do not make
a full account of the things
which my father hath written, for
he hath written many things which he
saw in visions and in dreams; and he
also hath written many things which
he prophesied and spake unto his
children, of which I shall not
make a full account."
(1 Nephi 1:16).

"I shall make an account
of my proceedings in my days.
Behold, I make an abridgement of the
record of my father, upon plates which
I have made with mine own hands;
wherefore, after I have abridged
the record of my father then
will I make an account
of mine own life."
(1 Nephi 1:17).

"He departed into the wilderness. And he left his house, and the land of his inheritance, and his gold, and his silver, and his precious things, and took nothing with him, save it were his family, and provisions, and tents, and (he) departed into the wilderness." (1 Nephi 2:4).

"Thy brothers murmur, saying it is a hard thing which I have required of them; but behold I have not required it of them, but it is a commandment of the Lord. Therefore go, my son, and thou shalt be favored of the Lord, because thou hast not murmured." (1 Nephi 3:5-6).

"Let us be faithful in keeping the commandments of the Lord; therefore, let us go down to the land of our father's inheritance, for behold he left gold and silver, and all manner of riches. And all this he hath done because of the commandments of the Lord."
(1 Nephi 3:16).

"And now I, Nephi, do not give the genealogy of my fathers in this part of my record; neither at any time shall I give it after upon these plates which I am writing; for it is given in the record which has been kept by my father; wherefore, I do not write it in this work." (1 Nephi 6:1).

"I looked and beheld
the Lamb of God, that he was
taken by the people; yea, the Son of
the everlasting God was judged of the
world; and I saw and bear record."
(1 Nephi 11:32).

"And while the angel
spake these words, I beheld and
saw that the seed of my brethren did
contend against my seed, according to
the word of the angel; and because of the
pride of my seed, and the temptations of
the devil, I beheld that the seed of my
brethren did overpower the people
of my seed." (1 Nephi 12:19).
"The time cometh that he

shall manifest himself unto
all nations, both unto the Jews and
also unto the Gentiles; and after he has
manifested himself unto the Jews and also
unto the Gentiles, then he shall manifest
himself unto the Gentiles and also unto
the Jews, and the last shall be first,
and the first shall be last."
(1 Nephi 13:42).

"I, Nephi, did exhort them to give heed unto the word of the Lord; yea, I did exhort them with all the energies of my soul, and with all the faculty which I possessed, that they would give heed to the word of God."
(1 Nephi 15:25).

"It came to pass that as I, Nephi, went forth to slay food, behold, I did break my bow, which was made of fine steel; and after I did break my bow, behold, my brethren were angry with me because of the loss of my bow, for we did obtain no food."
(1 Nephi 16:18).

"And I will also be
your light in the wilderness;
and I will prepare the way before
you, if it so be that ye shall keep my
commandments; wherefore, inasmuch
as ye shall keep my commandments
ye shall be led towards the promised
land; and ye shall know that it
is by me that ye are led."
(1 Nephi 17:13).

"Hearken, O ye house
of Israel, all ye that are broken
off and are driven out because of the
wickedness of the pastors of my people;
yea, all ye that are broken off, that
are scattered abroad, who are of
my people, O house of Israel."
(1 Nephi 21:1).

"Because of the righteousness of his
people, Satan has no power; wherefore, he
cannot be loosed for the space of many
years; for he hath no power over the
hearts of the people, for they
dwell in righteousness."
(1 Nephi 22:26).

"I will not put my
trust in the arm of flesh;
for I know that cursed is he
that putteth his trust in the arm
of flesh. Yea, cursed is he that
putteth his trust in man, or
maketh flesh his arm."
(2 Nephi 4:34).

"The words of the
Lord had been fulfilled unto my
brethren, which he spake concerning
them, that I should be their ruler and their
teacher. Wherefore, I had been their ruler
and their teacher, according to the
commandments of the Lord."
(2 Nephi 5:19).

"Behold, God is
my salvation; I will
trust, and not be afraid,
for the Lord Jehovah is my
strength and my song; he also
has become my salvation."
(2 Nephi 22:2).

"How art thou
fallen from heaven, O Lucifer,
son of the morning! Art thou cut down
to the ground, which did weaken the nations!
For thou hast said in thy heart: I will ascend into
heaven, I will exalt my throne above the stars of God;
I will sit also upon the mount of the congregation,
in the sides of the north; I will ascend above the
heights of the clouds; I will be like the Most
High. Yet thou shalt be brought down
to hell, to the sides of the pit."
(2 Nephi 24:12-15).

"And
others will
he pacify, and
lull them away into
carnal security, that they
will say: All is well in Zion;
yea, Zion prospereth, all is well,
and thus, the devil cheateth their
souls, and leadeth them away
carefully down to hell."
(2 Nephi 28:21).

"The Jews
shall have the words of
the Nephites, and the Nephites
shall have the words of the Jews;
and the Nephites and the Jews shall
have the words of the lost tribes of
Israel; and the lost tribes of Israel
shall have the words of the
Nephites and the Jews."
(2 Nephi 29:13).

"Thy faith
hath made the whole. Now it
came to pass that when I had heard these
words, I began to feel a desire for the welfare
of my brethren, the Nephites; wherefore, I did
pour out my whole soul unto God for them. And I
prayed unto him with many long strugglings
for my brethren, the Lamanites. And it came
to pass that after I had prayed and labored
with all diligence, the Lord said unto me:
I will grant unto thee according to thy
desires, because of thy faith."
(Enos 1:8,9 & 11,12).

"I soon go to the place of my rest, which is with my Redeemer; for I know that in him I shall rest. And I rejoice in the day when my mortal shall put on immortality, and shall stand before him; then shall I see his face with pleasure, and he will say unto me: Come unto me, ye blessed, there is a place prepared for you in the mansions of my Father."
(Enos 1:27).

"As many as are not stiffnecked and have faith, have communion with the Holy Spirit, which maketh manifest unto the children of men, according to their faith."
(Jarom 1:4).

"For this multitude being so great that King Benjamin could not teach them all within the walls of the temple, therefore, he caused a tower to be erected, that thereby his people might hear the words which he should speak unto them. And it came to pass that he began to speak to his people from the tower; and they could not all hear his words because of the greatness of the multitude; therefore, he caused that the words which he spake should be written and sent forth among those that were not under the sound of his voice, that they might also receive his words." (Mosiah 2:7-8).

"Men drink damnation to their own souls except they humble themselves and become as little children, and believe that salvation was, and is, and is to come, in and through the atoning blood of Christ, the Lord Omnipotent. For the natural man is an enemy to God, and has been from the fall of Adam, and will be, forever and ever, unless he yields to the enticings of the Holy Spirit, and putteth off the natural man and becometh a saint through the atonement of Christ the Lord, and becometh as a child." (Mosiah 3:18-19).

"See that all these things are done in wisdom and order; for it is not requisite that a man should run faster than he has strength. And again, it is expedient that he should be diligent, that thereby he might win the prize; therefore, all things must be done in order."
(Mosiah 4:27).

"And now, because of the covenant which ye have made, ye shall be called the children of Christ, his sons, and his daughters; for behold, this day he hath spiritually begotten you; for ye say that your hearts are changed through faith on his name; therefore, ye are born of him and have become his sons and his daughters."
(Mosiah 5:7).

"Whosoever shall
not take upon him
the name of Christ must
be called by some other name;
therefore, he findeth himself on the
left hand of God. And I would that ye
should remember also, that this is the name
that I said I should give unto you that never
should be blotted out of your hearts. I say unto
you, I would that ye should remember to retain the
name written always in your hearts, that ye are
not found on the left hand of God, but that
ye hear and know the voice by which ye
shall be called, and also the name
by which he shall call you."
(Mosiah 5:10-12).

"I will visit
them in my anger.
Yea, in my fierce anger
will I visit them."
(Mosiah 12:1).

"It is not expedient that we should have a king; for thus saith the Lord: Ye shall not esteem one flesh above another, or one man shall not think himself above another; therefore, I say unto you it is not expedient that ye should have a king."
(Mosiah 23:7).

"Four of them were the sons of Mosiah; and their names were Ammon, and Aaron, and Omner, and Himni; these were the names of the sons of Mosiah."
(Mosiah 27:34).

"He did deliver them because they did humble themselves before him; and because they cried mightily unto him he did deliver them out of bondage."
(Mosiah 29:20).

"Did not my father Alma
believe in the words which were
delivered by the mouth of Abinadi?
And was he not a holy prophet?
Did he not speak the words
of God, and my father
Alma believe them?"
(Alma 5:11).

"They are made known
unto me by the Holy Spirit of God.
Behold, I have fasted and prayed many
days that I might know these things of
myself. And now I do know of myself
that they are true; for the Lord God
hath made them manifest unto
me by his Holy Spirit."
(Alma 5:46).

"The angel said unto me, he
is a holy man; wherefore
I know he is a holy man
because it was said by
an angel of God."
(Alma 10:9).

"Zeezrom lay sick at
Sidom, with a burning fever,
which was caused by the great
tribulations of his mind on account
of his wickedness, for he supposed that
Alma and Amulek were no more; and he
supposed that they had been slain because
of his iniquity. And this great sin, and his
many other sins, did harrow up his mind
until it did become exceedingly sore,
having no deliverance; therefore,
he began to be scorched with
a burning heat."
(Alma 15:3).

"He had
slain many of them, because
their brethren had scattered their
flocks at the place of water; and
thus, because they had had
their flocks scattered,
they were slain."
(Alma 18:6).

"Now when Alma had said these words, Korihor was struck dumb, that he could not have utterance, according to the words of Alma." (Alma 30:50).

"For it is expedient that an atonement should be made; for according to the great plan of the Eternal God there must be an atonement made, or else all mankind must unavoidably perish; yea, all are hardened; yea, all are fallen and are lost, and must perish except it be through the atonement which it is expedient should be made." (Alma 34:9).

"For
it is expedient
that there should be
a great and last sacrifice;
yea, not a sacrifice of man,
neither of beast, neither of
any manner of fowl; for
it shall not be a human
sacrifice; but it must
be an infinite and
eternal sacrifice."
(Alma 34:10).

"Now Alma, being grieved
for the iniquity of his people, yea
for the wars, and the bloodsheds, and
the contentions which were among them;
and having been to declare the word, or sent
to declare the word, among all the people in
every city; and seeing that the hearts of the
people began to wax hard, and that they
began to be offended because of the
strictness of the word, his heart
was exceedingly sorrowful."
(Alma 35:15).

"Now the land south was called Lehi, and the land north was called Mulek, which was after the son of Zedekiah; for the Lord did bring Mulek into the land north, and Lehi into the land south." (Helaman 6:10).

"Behold, now we will know of a surety whether this man be a prophet and God hath commanded him to prophesy such marvelous things unto us. Behold, we do not believe that he hath; yea, we do not believe that he is a prophet; nevertheless, if this thing which he has said concerning the chief judge be true, that he be dead, then will we believe that the other words which he has spoken are true." (Helaman 9:2).

"Behold, I give unto you power, that whatsoever ye shall seal on earth shall be sealed in heaven; and whatsoever ye shall loose on earth shall be loosed in heaven; and thus shall ye have power among this people."
(Helaman 10:7).

"If we should go up against them, the Lord would deliver us into their hands; therefore, we will prepare ourselves in the center of our lands, and we will gather all our armies together, and we will not go against them, but we will wait till they shall come against us; therefore, as the Lord liveth, if we do this he will deliver them into our hands."
(3 Nephi 3:21).

"Your
burnt offerings
shall be done away,
for I will accept none
of your sacrifices and
your burnt offerings."
(3 Nephi 9:19).

"And it was the
more righteous part of
the people who were saved,
and it was they who received
the prophets and stoned them not;
and it was they who had not shed
the blood of the saints, who were
spared." (3 Nephi 10:12).

"He that
hath the spirit of
contention is not of me,
but is of the devil, who is the
father of contention, and he
stirreth up the hearts of men
to contend with anger, one
with another." (3 Nephi
11:29).

"No man can serve two masters; for either he will hate the one and love the other, or else he will hold to the one and despise the other. Ye cannot serve God and Mammon." (3 Nephi 13:24).

"I would speak somewhat unto the remnant of this people who are spared if it so be that God may give unto them my words, that they may know of the things of their fathers; yea, I speak unto you, ye remnant of the house of Israel; and these are the words which I speak." (Mormon 7:1).

"Are not
the things
that God hath
wrought marvelous
in our eyes? Yea, and
who can comprehend the
marvelous works of God?"
(Mormon 9:16).

"It was by faith that
the three disciples obtained a
promise that they should not taste
of death; and they obtained not the
promise until after their faith."
(Ether 12:17).

"I, Mormon, speak unto you, my
beloved brethren; and it is by the
grace of God the Father, and our
Lord Jesus Christ, and his holy
will, because of the gift of his
calling unto me, that I am
permitted to speak unto
you at this time."
(Moroni 7:2).

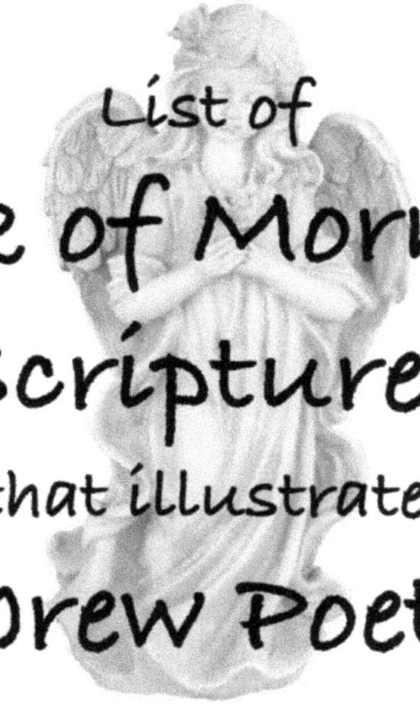

List of Book of Mormon Scriptures that illustrate Hebrew Poetry

While most poems in
English are governed by rhyme
and meter, Hebrew poetry is written
in free verse, with neither rhyme nor
meter. Instead, they are characterized
by "couplets," or to put it simply,
pairs of poetic lines.
Hebraic literary patterns

identify important passages,
add emphasis to messages, define
and enlarge upon main points, and
help to make information memorable
by structuring the text in a way that
makes it easy to understand the
words of the prophets.

Synonymous Parallelism

1 Nephi 1:6-7	2 Nephi 4:11	Alma 34:32
1 Nephi 2:3	2 Nephi 4:35	Alma 37:5
1 Nephi 2:11	2 Nephi 7:3	Alma 40:23
1 Nephi 5:19	2 Nephi 8:3	Helaman 12:6
1 Nephi 8:2	2 Nephi 9:52	Helaman 13:11
1 Nephi 9:4	2 Nephi 15:20	Helaman 14:25
1 Nephi 11:11	2 Nephi 22:4	3 Nephi 2:1
1 Nephi 11:21	2 Nephi 25:15	3 Nephi 5:21
1 Nephi 11:32	2 Nephi 28:3	3 Nephi 6:18
1 Nephi 12:2	2 Nephi 30:16	3 Nephi 12:19
1 Nephi 12:4	Jacob 1:6	3 Nephi 16:20
1 Nephi 17:36	Omni 1:12-13	3 Nephi 20:39
1 Nephi 17:39	Words of Mormon 1:7	Mormon 1:1
1 Nephi 17:47	Mosiah 2:2	Mormon 1:2
1 Nephi 17:50	Mosiah 16:10	Mormon 3:15
1 Nephi 17:53-54	Mosiah 21:26	Mormon 3:16
1 Nephi 18:17-18	Mosiah 23:5	Mormon 4:5
1 Nephi 18:34	Mosiah 23:21	Mormon 9:9
1 Nephi 20:10	Mosiah 24:23	Mormon 9:10
1 Nephi 21:2	Alma 2:22	Ether 12:31
1 Nephi 21:9	Alma 5:45	Ether 14:2
1 Nephi 21:11	Alma 8:4	Moroni 2:7
1 Nephi 21:14	Alma 11:20	Moroni 7:13
1 Nephi 21:24	Alma 25:12	Moroni 8:17
2 Nephi 1:13	Alma 27:22	Moroni 10:6

Hebrew poetry
illustrates in its
own inimitable and
beautiful way why we
must consecrate our lives
to our Savior Jesus Christ
by throwing ourselves upon
an altar of sacrifice whose
foundation is buttressed
by a supernal display
of divine direction
from above.

Over the years, "The Book of Mormon
has been read in many ways by those who
seek to apply its messages to their lives, as well as
by those who wish to delve into its ancient origins. It
submits itself openly to all kinds of rhetorical analyses,
theological discussions, and comparative literary studies.
But above all, no matter how it is read, The Book of Mormon
welcomes readers, inviting them to meet its prophets and to
be transformed by its wisdom. It begs to be read."
(John W. Welch, "Poetic Parallelisms in
The Book of Mormon").

Antithetical Parallelism

1 Nephi 2:20-21	2 Nephi 3:17	Alma 1:25
1 Nephi 6:5	2 Nephi 4:4	Alma 5:40
1 Nephi 13:18	2 Nephi 4:19	Alma 9:13
1 Nephi 14:7	2 Nephi 4:33	Alma 9:28
1 Nephi 14:25	2 Nephi 9:16	Alma 22:6
1 Nephi 15:3	2 Nephi 9:23-24	Alma 33:21
1 Nephi 15:8-9	2 Nephi 9:39	Alma 36:20
1 Nephi 16:3	2 Nephi 12:5	Alma 36:21
2 Nephi 13:24	2 Nephi 12:7	Helaman 7:29
2 Nephi 15:12	2 Nephi 1:7	3 Nephi 13:34
2 Nephi 15:15-16	2 Nephi 16:10	3 Nephi 14:13
2 Nephi 16:9	2 Nephi 18:10	3 Nephi 20:42
1 Nephi 16:29	2 Nephi 18:19	3 Nephi 27:33
1 Nephi 17:6	2 Nephi 19:2	Mormon 1:16
1 Nephi 17:37	2 Nephi 21:3-4	Mormon 2:13
1 Nephi 17:38	2 Nephi 25:20	Mormon 2:14
1 Nephi 17:45	2 Nephi 33:8	Mormon 2:26
1 Nephi 19:7	Jacob 1:14	Ether 4:18
1 Nephi 21:7	Jacob 6:3	Ether 12:12
2 Nephi 1:20	Omni 1:3	Ether 12:25
2 Nephi 1:25	Omni 1:25	Ether 12:26
2 Nephi 1:26	Mosiah 2:25	Moroni 7:11
2 Nephi 1:28-29	Mosiah 3:29	Moroni 7:16-17
2 Nephi 2:11	Mosiah 18:21	Moroni 7:42
2 Nephi 2:28-29	Mosiah 27:29	Moroni 8:8

Hebrew poetry in the Book of Mormon can infuse us with a knowledge of God's Plan, bringing us to the point that our "bodies shall be filled with light, and there shall be no darkness in (us); and that body which is filled with light comprehendeth all things."
(D&C 88:67).

Hebraic poetry in The Book of Mormon charges our vision with an illimitable perspective, wherein we may experience pulsing streams of insight, intuition, inspiration, and revelation, whose mighty ebb and flow has neither spatial nor temporal limitations.

Synthetic Parallelism

2 Nephi 2:25	2 Nephi 9:31-37	Mosiah 23:21
2 Nephi 3:15	2 Nephi 33:1	Helaman 12:7
2 Nephi 4:35	Jacob 5:2	Moroni 8:17

In a
perfect storm that
has been characterized
by our faith, belief, and
knowledge, the presence of
Hebrew poetry in The Book of
Mormon activates a switch that
distributes power to the twinkling
stars in the midst of the heavens,
whose inexhaustible celestial fuel,
in turn, feeds a chain reaction
in the nuclear furnace of
creation itself.

Hebraic
poetry in The Book
of Mormon re-acquaints
us with God's divine design
as we put the finishing touches
on our dissertations on life. As He
perfects us, our compositions go thru
an evolution until they reach the point
where they may be recognized for what
they have become. Each is a genuine
magnum opus, and when they are
taken as a whole, they represent
an incarnation of His work
and His glory.

Climactic Parallelism

1 Nephi 2:5	2 Nephi 5:7	Alma 16:1
1 Nephi 3:7	2 Nephi 5:25	Alma 31:5
1 Nephi 7:10-12	2 Nephi 9:6-7	Alma 32:12
1 Nephi 9:6	2 Nephi 9:12	Alma 32:13
1 Nephi 10:2-3	2 Nephi 9:25	Alma 32:14
1 Nephi 10:19	2 Nephi 9:26	Alma 36:4
1 Nephi 15:33	2 Nephi 10:3	Alma 42:14
1 Nephi 16:20	2 Nephi 20:17	Helaman 10:6
1 Nephi 17:19	2 Nephi 21:12	3 Nephi 6:13
1 Nephi 17:31	2 Nephi 23:10	3 Nephi 8:16
1 Nephi 18:2	2 Nephi 25:24-27	3 Nephi 10:15
1 Nephi 18:22	2 Nephi 29:12	Mormon 3:9-10
1 Nephi 19:15-17	2 Nephi 30:11	Mormon 3:12
1 Nephi 19:24	2 Nephi 33:6	Mormon 8:14
1 Nephi 20:18	Jacob 4:10	Ether 2:17
1 Nephi 20:21	Enos 1:4-5	Ether 4:12
2 Nephi 1:5	Mosiah 2:17	Ether 12:27
2 Nephi 1:13-14	Mosiah 10:17	Ether 12:32
2 Nephi 2:5-6	Mosiah 11:28	Ether 13:17
2 Nephi 2:6-9	Mosiah 16:12	Ether 14:1
2 Nephi 2:13	Mosiah 22:4	Moroni 7:8
2 Nephi 2:18	Mosiah 27:14	Moroni 7:35
2 Nephi 2:27	Mosiah 29:40	Moroni 7:44 & 46
2 Nephi 4:15-16	Alma 5:37	Moroni 10:32
2 Nephi 4:30	Alma 7:12	Moroni 10:33

During the
past half century, the work
of outstanding L.D.S. scholars has
introduced those who study The Book of
Mormon to myriad Hebraic literary devices,
the most famous of which is chiasmus. But
chiasmus has many literary cousins that
are worth getting to know. Examples,
as it turns out, can be found on
nearly every page of the text.

There is no parallel figure of speech
that is more important than the chief message of The
Book of Mormon, which is to convince both "Jew and Gentile that
Jesus is the Christ, the Eternal God." (Book of Mormon Title Page).
And yet, "all of these forms and figures are designed to present this
message regarding Jesus Christ and his gospel in an unforgettable,
understandable, artistic, and fascinating way. These forms and
figures gave writers of scripture unique methods of expression
as they set forth religious doctrines, tenets, and principles.
Apparently, the prophets and writers of the scriptures
employed the repetition of alternating parallel
lines for the purpose of reinforcing their
teachings and doctrines." (Donald
W. Parry, "Poetic Parallelisms in
The Book of Mormon").

Chiasmus

1 Nephi 1:1-3	1 Nephi 13:29-30	2 Nephi 3:1
1 Nephi 1:15-18	1 Nephi 13:39-42	2 Nephi 5:2-4
1 Nephi 1:20-2:1	1 Nephi 14:15-16	2 Nephi 5:16
1 Nephi 2:2-5	1 Nephi 14:20-25	2 Nephi 5:25
1 Nephi 2:11-12	1 Nephi 15:7-8	2 Nephi 6:13
1 Nephi 3:1-2	1 Nephi 15:24	2 Nephi 6:14-15
1 Nephi 3:16-22	1 Nephi 15:25	2 Nephi 6:16-17
1 Nephi 4:5-24	1 Nephi 16:1-3	2 Nephi 7:1
1 Nephi 4:32	1 Nephi 16:13-14	2 Nephi 8:11
1 Nephi 4:33-35	1 Nephi 16:28-29	2 Nephi 8:15
1 Nephi 5:7-9	1 Nephi 17:7	2 Nephi 8:19
1 Nephi 5:14-16	1 Nephi 17:13	2 Nephi 9:20
1 Nephi 5:17-20	1 Nephi 17:18-19	2 Nephi 9:28
1 Nephi 6:1-2	1 Nephi 17:31	2 Nephi 9:38
1 Nephi 7:3-5	1 Nephi 17:38	2 Nephi 9:42
1 Nephi 7:13	1 Nephi 17:48-52	2 Nephi 9:44-46
1 Nephi 7:16-19	1 Nephi 17:52	2 Nephi 11:2-8
1 Nephi 8:8-9	1 Nephi 18:24	2 Nephi 12:3
1 Nephi 8:10-12	1 Nephi 19:13-14	2 Nephi 12:10-19
1 Nephi 8:22-23	1 Nephi 20:21	2 Nephi 15:7
1 Nephi 9:3-5	1 Nephi 21:1	2 Nephi 15:25
1 Nephi 11:11	1 Nephi 21:11	2 Nephi 16:10
1 Nephi 11:16-22	1 Nephi 21:24-25	2 Nephi 17:10-12
1 Nephi 11:32	1 Nephi 22:1-3	2 Nephi 18:17
1 Nephi 11:34-35	1 Nephi 22:25	2 Nephi 19:21
1 Nephi 12:19	2 Nephi 1:13-23	2 Nephi 20:20-21
1 Nephi 13:16-19	2 Nephi 1:28-29	2 Nephi 20:24
1 Nephi 13:26	2 Nephi 2:7	2 Nephi 21:4

2 Nephi 22:2	Mosiah 7:4	Alma 18:7
2 Nephi 24:9-18	Mosiah 7:7-8	Alma 18:12-14
2 Nephi 24:29-31	Mosiah 8:17	Alma 18:16
2 Nephi 25:4	Mosiah 10:17	Alma 18:38
2 Nephi 25:7	Mosiah 11:20-25	Alma 18:39
2 Nephi 25:15	Mosiah 11:28	Alma 19:6-7
2 Nephi 25:24-27	Mosiah 12:1-8	Alma 19:13
2 Nephi 26:1-9	Mosiah 12:19	Alma 20:10-13
2 Nephi 27:1-4	Mosiah 12:24	Alma 20:26-27
2 Nephi 27:5	Mosiah 12:25	Alma 26:29
2 Nephi 28:3	Mosiah 14:7	Alma 27:22
2 Nephi 28:16-20	Mosiah 15:20-24	Alma 29:1-7
2 Nephi 28:21	Mosiah 15:26-27	Alma 29:8-17
2 Nephi 28:32	Mosiah 15:31	Alma 30:4-5
2 Nephi 29:3-6	Mosiah 16:7-8	Alma 30:6-12
2 Nephi 29:13	Mosiah 18:1-3	Alma 30:44
2 Nephi 30:9	Mosiah 18:21	Alma 30:50-52
2 Nephi 32:2	Mosiah 24:14-15	Alma 30:17-23
Jacob 1:11	Mosiah 24:21	Alma 31:31-33
Jacob 1:14	Mosiah 26:1-3	Alma 32:1
Jacob 2:6-10	Mosiah 26:21-28	Alma 32:5
Jacob 3:6	Mosiah 27:24-25	Alma 32:9-10
Jacob 4:9	Mosiah 27:34	Alma 32:12
Jacob 5:7-9	Mosiah 28:10-29:2	Alma 33:11
Jacob 5:46-47	Mosiah 29:20	Alma 34:9
Jacob 5:61-64	Alma 1:1	Alma 34:10
Jacob 7:19	Alma 2:22	Alma 34:11-12
Enos 1:8-12	Alma 3:6-7	Alma 34:13-14
Enos 1:13-16	Alma 5:7-9	Alma 34:34
Jarom 1:1-15	Alma 5::20-25	Alma 34:36
Omni 1:5-7	Alma 5:44-49	Alma 35:15
Omni 1:12-13	Alma 5:62	Alma 36:1-30
Omni 1:14	Alma 6:5	Alma 37:1-13
Mosiah 2:5-6	Alma 7:11-13	Alma 37:21-26
Mosiah 2:7-8	Alma 8:4	Alma 37:35
Mosiah 2 15-16	Alma 9:12	Alma 40:23
Mosiah 2:25	Alma 9:31-32	Alma 41:10-12
Mosiah 2:26	Alma 10:7-11	Alma 41:13-14
Mosiah 3:1-3	Alma 11:40	Alma 42:5-8
Mosiah 3:11-16	Alma 12:11-17	Alma 42:13
Mosiah 3:18-19	Alma 13:2-3	Alma 42:14
Mosiah 4:6-7	Alma 13:6-10	Alma 42:15
Mosiah 4:11-12	Alma 14:2-3	Alma 43:38
Mosiah 4:14-15	Alma 14:29	Alma 46:24
Mosiah 4:18-23	Alma 15:3	Alma 49:2-3
Mosiah 5:8-9	Alma 16:1	Alma 49:18-19
Mosiah 5:10-12	Alma 18:6	Alma 49:26-27

Alma 50:14	Helaman 14:23	3 Nephi 25:1
Alma 52:3	Helaman 15:3	3 Nephi 25:5-6
Alma 52:28-31	Helaman 16:2-3	3 Nephi 26:16-18
Alma 53:1	3 Nephi 1:15	3 Nephi 27:7-9
Alma 53:8-9	3 Nephi 1:25	3 Nephi 27:13
Alma 54:12	3 Nephi 2:7-8	3 Nephi 27:19
Alma 56:38	3 Nephi 4:15	3 Nephi 28:1-4
Alma 57:25-26	3 Nephi 4:24-25	3 Nephi 28:13-14
Alma 60:15-16	3 Nephi 5:8	4 Nephi 1:31-34
Alma 60:22	3 Nephi 5:24-26	Mormon 1:16
Alma 61:12-13	3 Nephi 6:1-2	Mormon 2:8
Alma 63:11-13	3 Nephi 6:13	Mormon 9:10
Helaman 1:3-4	3 Nephi 6:18	Mormon 9:13
Helaman 2:1-2	3 Nephi 6:20	Mormon 9:15
Helaman 3:13-15	3 Nephi 7:2-4	Mormon 9:18
Helaman 3:24-26	3 Nephi 8:10	Mormon 9:19
Helaman 4:9-19	3 Nephi 8:16	Mormon 9:32-33
Helaman 5:48-50	3 Nephi 9:16-17	Ether 1:5
Helaman 6:7-13	3 Nephi 9:19	Ether 1:35
Helaman 6:10	3 Nephi 10:4-5	Ether 1:38
Helaman 6:15	3 Nephi 10:12	Ether 3:4-5
Helaman 6:21-26	3 Nephi 10:12	Ether 3:19-20
Helaman 7:1-3	3 Nephi 11:5-8	Ether 6:9
Helaman 7:6-9	3 Nephi 11:29	Ether 6:14-20
Helaman 7:29	3 Nephi 12:10-12	Ether 10:23
Helaman 8:20	3 Nephi 12:19	Ether 12:7
Helaman 8:27	3 Nephi 12:23-25	Ether 12:17
Helaman 10:4-5	3 Nephi 12:42	Ether 12:23-25
Helaman 10:7	3 Nephi 13:22	Ether 12:32
Helaman 10:13-15	3 Nephi 13:24	Ether 13:4-6
Helaman 11:2	3 Nephi 13:34	Ether 13:12
Helaman 11:5-6	3 Nephi 15:17-21	Moroni 1:2-3
Helaman 11:21	3 Nephi 16:20	Moroni 1:4
Helaman 13:5-9	3 Nephi 17:6-7	Moroni 2:1-3
Helaman 13:11	3 Nephi 17:12-13	Moroni 4:1
Helaman 13:20	3 Nephi 17:24	Moroni 7:11
Helaman 13:24-25	3 Nephi 18:22	Moroni 7:14
Helaman 13:27	3 Nephi 18:27-35	Moroni 7:27-29
Helaman 14:2-8	3 Nephi 19:2-3	Moroni 9:22
Helaman 14:15-17	3 Nephi 20:35	Moroni 10:4-5
Helaman 14:21-22	3 Nephi 23:3	

"Rarely in Book of Mormon studies has a concept captured our imagination more than the presence of chiasmus in its narratives. That fascination is only enhanced by the full array of other kinds of parallelistic structures present on its pages. Many people who have been inclined initially to discount the book as superficial or as insubstantial have felt required, when confronted by the presence of sophisticated literary forms in texts such as King Benjamin's speech, to back up a few giant steps and think much more deeply about the book, its origins, and its messages." (John W. Welch, "Poetic Parallelisms in The Book of Mormon").

For those who are adventurous enough to tackle reading the entire Book of Mormon with its multitudinous parallelisms comprehensively documented and annotated in a readable fashion, I highly recommend the following scholarly work: "Poetic Parallelisms in The Book of Mormon," Donald W. Parry, Brigham Young University, BYU Scholars Archive, Maxwell Institute Publications, 2007.

Cognates
In The Book of Mormon

Cognates are related words that come from the same root. For example, the English noun 'student' is cognate to the verb 'study' and to the adjective 'studious'. In Hebrew, a verb is sometimes followed by a noun that is a cognate, such as "wrote upon it a writing" (Exodus 39:30), or "she vowed a vow" (1 Samuel 1:11), and sometimes, the verb and the noun are the same word. "I will work a great and a marvelous work" (1 Nephi 14:7).

When writing in English, cognates are used infrequently, because they are considered awkward, or inelegant in their style. For example, someone writing in English would be more likely to use "thy servant vowed" or "he made a vow," rather than "thy servant vowed a vow." (1 Samuel 15:8).

A cognate accusative is a device that arises from the similarity between related Hebrew words. For example, the words Jershon, inheritance, and possession, that are found in Alma Chapter 27. "And they went down into the land of Jershon, and took possession (YRS) of the land of Jershon" (yarsôn) "for an inheritance" (yarsôn, Alma 27:22). This is a remarkable example of the cognate accusative in the underlying Hebrew text of The Book of Mormon.

In many ways The Book of Mormon sounds like a Hebrew text. John A. Tvedtnes has pointed out that The Book of Mormon employs cognates more than would be expected if the original language of the book had been English. These cognates illustrate the book's Hebrew influence. One of the most widely recognized examples is the familiar "I have dreamed a dream" (1 Nephi 8:2). That is exactly the way the same idea is expressed in literal translations from Old Testament Hebrew. It looks like Joseph Smith has scored another bullseye! (See Genesis 37:5 & 41:11).

Cognates in The Book of Mormon include the following 23 examples, each followed by the more comfortable expression as it might typically be rendered in English.

"I will curse them even with a sore curse" (1 Nephi 2:23), instead of "I will curse them sorely."

"I have dreamed a dream" (1 Nephi 3:2), instead of "I have had a dream."

"I have dreamed a dream" (1 Nephi 8:2), instead of "I have had a dream."

It "yoketh them with a yoke of iron" (1 Nephi 13:5), instead of "it burdens them with a yoke of iron."

"I will work a great and a marvelous work" (1 Nephi 14:7), instead of "I will perform a great and marvelous work."

"Arise from the dust ... that ye may not be cursed with a sore cursing" (2 Nephi 1:22), instead of "Arise from the dust ... that ye may not be sorely cursed."

"I did teach the people to build buildings" (2 Nephi 5:15), instead of "I did teach the people to construct buildings."

"They are cursed with a sore cursing" (Jacob 3:3), instead of "They are sorely cursed."

"This was the desire which I desired of him" (Enos 1:13), instead of "This is what I desired of him."

"Succor those that stand in need of your succor" (Mosiah 4:16), instead of "Comfort those that stand in need of your succor."

"(We are) taxed with a tax" (Mosiah 7:15), instead of "We are "taxed."

"And we began to build buildings" (Mosiah 9:8), instead of "And we began to construct buildings."

"He also caused that his workmen should work all manner of fine work" (Mosiah 11:10), instead of " He also caused that his workmen should create all manner of things."

"He caused many buildings to be built" (Mosiah 11:13), instead of "He caused many buildings to be constructed."

They began "to build buildings" (Mosiah 23:5), instead of "They began to erect buildings," or "They began to construct buildings."

"Judge a righteous judgment" (Mosiah 29:29), instead of "Make a righteous judgment."

"He did judge righteous judgments" (Mosiah 29:43), instead of "He judged righteously" or "He made righteous judgments."

"Have ye felt to sing the song of redeeming love?" (Alma 5:26), instead of "Have ye felt to sing about redeeming love?"

"Limoni began to fear exceedingly, with fear" (Alma 18:5), instead of "Limoni began to fear exceedingly."

"Behold, We will give up the land of Jershon, which is on the east by the sea, which joins the land Bountiful, which is on the south of the land Bountiful; and this land Jershon is the land which we will give unto our brethren for an inheritance." (Alma 27:22), instead of "We will give unto our brethren for an inheritance the land of Jershon, which is on the east by the sea, which is on the south of the land Bountiful."

"They went down into the land of Jershon, and took possession of the land of Jershon." (Alma 27:26), instead of "They went down into the land of Jershon, and took possession of it."

"This people is a free people" (Alma 30:24), instead of "These people are free."

"And they did work all manner of fine work (Ether 10:23), instead of "And they did engage in all manner of fine work."

Weak and insipid claims
that Joseph Smith composed the
Book of Mormon by simply imitating
the King James English, using some biblical
names while inventing others, typically exhibit
insensitivity and ignorance relating to its myriad
linguistic nuances. The use of cognates scattered
throughout the text would render the fabrication
of the book an overwhelming challenge for
anyone in Joseph Smith's day, let
alone for an untutored lad
such as he.

Observations

The day that was foreseen by Mormon is now at hand, when "every ear shall hear it, and every knee shall bow, and every tongue shall confess" that Jesus is the Christ. (D&C 88:104). He will be recognized as the "Lord of lords, and King of kings." (Rev. 17:14). When we invite Him to come and dwell in our hearts, He becomes not only the finisher of our faith but also the author of our spiritual regeneration, as well as the poet laureate of our Heavenly Father.

We read in scripture that those who have repented and become the Lord's disciples are figuratively characterized as "white, fair, and beautiful." (1 Nephi 13:5). Moroni used the terms "spotless, pure, fair, and white."(Mormon 9:6). These are those who symbolically have been cleansed by the blood of the Lamb, in a rite of purification as old as time itself.

If Latter-day Nephites and Lamanites are ever going to inherit exaltation and enjoy eternal life with our Father in Heaven, they must do more than just acknowledge that Jesus is Lord. The critical point of conversion, beyond which lie the encircling flames of fire in the Celestial Kingdom of God, rests in making a conscious decision to accept not only the Savior, but also His gospel. A simple yet uncommitted recognition of Jesus does not qualify us to live with Him forever. Christians of convenience lack the fire that the demands of discipleship require. Only those who have passionately embraced the gospel with its ordinances and covenants, and who are subsequently mentored by the Master, are following a path that leads to the highest degree of glory within God's Celestial Kingdom, where they will live forever with His holy embrace.

Book of Mormon credos envelop us in an intuitive appreciation of where we have come from, the tangible element of why we are here, as well as the revelatory reassurance of where we are going.

Book of Mormon prophets have painted a vivid portrait of the miracles that are sure to occur in our lives if we will only turn our faces toward heaven. (See Alma 5:14 & 26). Although they will always be higher than ours, God's thoughts will have become our thoughts, and His ways will be our ways. (See Isaiah 55:8-9). We will be mesmerized by His work and His glory, and will be nudged ever closer to the mind-bending realization that, as Henri Bergson declared: the universe was created to be "a machine for the making of gods."

Those who have feasted upon The Book of Mormon by sinking their teeth into it and savoring it; who've prayed for help in digesting it, and have then sought to receive a witness that what they've devoured is true, know what spiritual hunger is. It's when the powers of heaven and earth amplify each other and lift us up on harmonic waves. When we experience moments like this, it's as if someone has given us gospel glasses to wear. Principles pop out, seeming to resonate more clearly. We feel as if we've been granted the eternal perspective that we've for so long been searching, that we might satisfy our craving for celestial certainties, and we determine to never again settle for Satan's telestial treats that cause carnal cavities and temporal toothaches.

It has never been
an easy thing to explain
to the uninitiated, who have not
yet received a testimony of The Book
of Mormon, how the Lord speaks to His
children. "The wind bloweth where it listeth,
and thou hearest the sound thereof, but canst
not tell whence it cometh, and whither it goeth.
So is every one that is born of the Spirit." (John
3:8). He has said His words are "not of men, nor of
man, but of me. Wherefore, you shall testify they
are of me, and not of man. For it is my voice which
speaketh them unto you; for they are given by my
Spirit unto you, and by my power you can read
them one to another; and save it were by my
power you could not have them. Wherefore
you can testify that you have heard
my voice, and know my words."
(D&C 18: 34-36).

Nephites
who were mired in
the bonds of iniquity
or in the quicksands of
sin knew on an intimate
basis what despair felt like.
It was the hopelessness they
felt when they had to deal with
the sense of futility that came
from having to choose between
alternatives that were equally
disappointing because they
were fruitless, or devoid
of value.

Alexander Pope's observation long ago rings true even today, that "vice is a monster of so frightful mien, as to be hated needs but to be seen. Yet seen too oft, familiar with her face, we first endure, then pity, then embrace." We must recognize that it is easier to hold up an umbrella than it is to turn off the rain. In our communities, some of which would rival Ammonihah in their depravity, it seems that immorality is often legislated. When this happens, it takes on a legitimacy it has neither earned nor deserves. Since wickedness cannot be summarily eliminated, the faithful need to take whatever measures may be necessary to initiate damage control as quickly as possible. The proven remedy is a healthy dose of gospel principles, together with a dash of sackcloth and ashes.

Just as the Lord Jehovah had sworn an oath with Noah that He would never again destroy the earth by a flood, so did He likewise swear in Bountiful that He wouldn't be angry with the children of Israel. "For the mountains shall depart and the hills be removed, but my kindness shall not depart from thee, neither shall the covenant of my peace be removed, saith the Lord that hath mercy on thee." (3 Nephi 22:10).

Anti-Christ is anyone who openly rebels against the Lord, and actively opposes Him. (See Alma Chapter 30). He may establish himself or any other person, system, or set of beliefs as a surrogate for the Savior, and then seek to promote his own alternative agenda. It is with a perverted, twisted reasoning that Anti-Christ attempts to overthrow true doctrine by preaching things that are flattering to those with itching ears. He often has formidable skills and weapons in his arsenal, but like the sophist, he is an intellectual guerilla, who insists on fighting his battles on his own turf and according to his own rules. He uses the persuasiveness of his dramatic oratory skills, his polished rhetoric, and the siren song of seduction as his most effective armaments, and they are typically economical in terms of tangible benefits. He has found that he does not need to use expensive high velocity large caliber armor piercing rounds in order to effectively kill our spirits. The fiery darts of vanity seem to be adequate to the task at hand.

Following the post-mortal ministry of Jesus Christ among the Nephites, those who lived their lives in daily thanksgiving opened up their eyes to the wonders and beauties of the world as if seeing them for the first time. By looking through rose-colored gospel glasses, they became the happiest people in all the earth. (See 4 Nephi 1:16).

When our Savior Jesus Christ returns to the earth, He will come in power, that alludes to His personal righteousness. (See Alma 5:50). He will come in dominion, suggesting priesthood authority. He will come in glory, worthy of the inner peace that righteousness brings. He will come in majesty, which submits that Christ is King of all the earth, that He exercises His power, and is in control of all things. He will come in might, which means that His strength is more than enough to vanquish Satan and to establish His dominion, which is the Kingdom of God on the earth.

When the threads that have been woven into the conduct of our lives are arranged in a pattern of holy vestments that've been established by the Savior, we'll embrace every tenet of The Book of Mormon, scales of darkness fall away, and the eyes of our spiritual understanding will be opened to the heavens. We will attune our ears, that we might comprehend the otherwise inaudible whisperings of the Spirit, and our hearts will be stirred with a pure love of Christ as we lose ourselves in service and show compassion toward our friends and neighbors.

Far too often, impatient Nephites developed an insatiable desire for telestially titillating fast food that had been carelessly prepared and then hastily heated up in a sensory microwave oven. It was of no nutritional value because, during its preparation, it was saturated with the empty calories of carnality. When unrepentant Nephites measured the messages delivered by the missionaries, they saw darkly, or only through the clouded filter of a worldly pollution. Their fruitless attempts to whitewash the truth did nothing but highlight the underlying sores that were a corruption and a canker on their character, and that only served to blind them even further to the truth.

We've been blessed with the principles and the doctrine of The Book of Mormon because God knows that there will be times when we will be tempted to step in and try to make up the rules ourselves. It was for this reason that He has provided us with His undeviating celestial standard. It is absolute and allows no exceptions. There is no wiggle room. It is complete obedience to the principles of the gospel, pure and simple, and nothing less will be tolerated of those who wish to enjoy the hearth, home, and hospitality of His kingdom.

The Book of
Mormon is God's gift to the
world, that the terrible indictment
of the wicked in the Last Days might
be lifted. As it stands, they can have no
claim on the Lord's tender mercies, because
they have either willfully or ignorantly made
the decision to deny themselves the blessings of
the Atonement. (See 1 Nephi 1:20). In their case, the
Final Judgment has already taken place as they begin
to realize that it will be a very unpleasant experience, as
an awful avalanche of consequences overwhelms them,
smothering any hope of timely deliverance. They will
have rolled the dice, counting on lady-luck, but they
will have lost everything in an ill-considered wager
with fate. When they are finally given over to the
buffetings of Satan, they will be permitted, on
their own initiative, to scrape together their
very last farthings to, in some way, make
a late payment to Justice for their
redemption.

Those with the
faith to have become
the beneficiaries of God's
divine intervention, and who
have put Moroni's challenge to
the test, have been touched by
angels, and have in many
other ways been blessed
to walk in the light
of the Lord.

Those who have been characterized as being stiff-necked have skin that is so thick and calloused that extraordinary measures are required to penetrate it, that their spirits might be touched. As Enos reported of his people: "There was nothing save it was exceeding harshness, preaching, and prophesying of wars, and contentions, and destructions, and continually reminding them of death, and the duration of eternity, and the judgments and the power of God, and all these things, stirring them up continually to keep them in the fear of the Lord; I say there was nothing short of these things, and exceedingly great plainness of speech, would keep them from going down speedily to destruction." (Enos 1:23).

As covenant Israel is gathered to the stakes of Zion from the four corners of the earth during the Last Days, the testimonies of individual members of The Church of Jesus Christ will ignite with the flame of faith as the Lord blesses them with the spiritual tools they will need to tap into their potential. (See 2 Nephi 21:12). To reach God's kingdom, they must set their course, and then move along it. Their progression will begin with small steps. Life will be as a sheet of paper white, where each of us may write a line or two, and then comes night. We must greatly begin, and if, as fate would have it, we have time but for a line, we need at least to make that one small shining moment in Camelot sublime. Not failure, but low aim is crime. (See "Life," James Russell Lowell).

It is in The Book
of Mormon where we learn that
every member of the human family
is a precious child of God who has been
invited to participate in the organizations
through which Jesus Christ governs His church.
But it's only those who have become Saints, those
who've been bound by its ordinances, who may receive
all of the promised blessings of the gospel by means of
covenants of action between themselves and the Lord.
(See Mosiah 3:19). Ordinances attest to the nature
of God and they confirm that The Church of Jesus
Christ is founded on unchanging principles.
They bridge the gulf between heaven and
earth, reassuring us that conditions
for obtaining salvation are
the same for all.

When we defy
Satan and we stand up to
him by remaining true to our
covenants, He gets angry, as he was
with Moses during their confrontation on
"an exceedingly high mountain" so long ago.
(Moses 1:1). On that occasion, he cried with a loud
voice, trembled, and shook, but then departed from the
great lawgiver, who remained resolute at that pivotal point
in his personal progress. Things will be somewhat different
during the Millennium. "Because of the righteousness of his
people" who remain on the earth during those thousand years
of peace, Satan will be bound, and he will not "be loosed for
the space of many years; for he (will then have) no power
over the hearts of the people, for they (will) dwell in
righteousness, and the Holy One of Israel
reigneth." (1 Nephi 22:26).

In every age of the world, Nephites, reconverted Lamanites, and last but not least, Latter-day Saints, who have experienced persecution firsthand, have always gathered in their holy places to prepare themselves for a day when tribulation and "desolation (will be) sent forth upon the wicked." (D&C 29:8).

Before he is able to unceremoniously drag them kicking and screaming down to hell, Satan gently places a flaxen cord that actually feels quite comfortable around the necks of the imprudent. (See 2 Nephi 26:22). But once inappropriate behavior patterns have been established, the unwary are unpleasantly surprised to find that they have sacrificed their agency to act independently, and they are bound by the yoke of sin to engage in conduct that is habitually self-defeating but is very difficult to change. In this way will the adversary bind us with his strong chains forever, and squeeze the last vestiges of celestial air from our lungs.

When it is humming along at its full capacity, the perpetual motion machine that is The Book of Mormon generates a vigorous charge to our surroundings stimulating change. During that process, we are nourished at a smorgasbord where we never become satiated. When our lives are in harmony with gospel principles, we are in a constant state of improvement leading to perfection. It's as if we were experiencing night after night the delights of a five star restaurant, and awakening in the morning with our doctrinal digestion working perfectly, and our spiritual bodies even more fit and trim than they had been beforehand.

As we gird ourselves with the whole armour of God, we press forward with complete dedication, steadfastness, confidence, and a firm determination in Christ, with a perfect brightness of hope, or flawless faith, and charity, or a love of God and of our brothers and sisters. If we do this by not only casually sampling, but feasting upon the words of Christ, enduring in righteousness thru this veil of tears to the very end, we will have eternal life, which is the greatest gift that God may bestow. (See 2 Nephi 31:20).

By enlightened latter-day standards, we would consider it to be insane to put to death those who violate the Sabbath Day; yet we die spiritually when we estrange ourselves from God's influence, inasmuch as we have put our eternal progression on hold. (See Mosiah 13:17). Brigham Young felt that the dominion God gave to us was designed to test us, and to enable us to show just how we would act if entrusted with His power. He has created a special time of the week as a work release program that allows us to show Him how we might behave when left on our own, after having received instructions that pointedly teach us what we ought to be doing on this, His holy day.

A conduit of living water flowing through The Book of Mormon like a rushing torrent nurtures our testimonies when we have not only believed, but we have also acted upon our belief, by being honest, true, chaste, benevolent, virtuous, kind, and in doing good to others. Living water has the power to sustain our lives when we are doers, and not only hearers, of the word. (See James 1:22).

Each morning, as shafts of gold burst upon the world with the dawn of a new day and we rub the sleep from our eyes, we will be resolute as we persist in our determination to read another chapter or two in The Book of Mormon. Its influence will encourage us to conduct our affairs that we might always be honest, true, chaste, benevolent, virtuous, and do good to others. As our understanding increases, so will our capacity to see God's influence over every aspect of our lives. We will attempt to see adversity as a necessary and beneficial component of our experience. In times of trial, we will remember the Savior, Who descended beneath all things, and Who set the example for us. We'll be drawn to the light. It will become part of our nature to relate comfortably with that which is virtuous, lovely, of good report, and praiseworthy. Anything that charges our souls, creates a nurturing atmosphere, or encourages us to improvement, will be worthy of our pursuit.

When we feast upon the words of Christ as they are found within The Book of Mormon, we will receive health in our navels and marrow in our bones (see D&C 89:18), strength in our loins as well as our sinews, (see Job 40:16-17), and power in the priesthood, (see D&C 107:14). As we receive nourishment from the scriptures, we will be fortified to endure to the end in righteousness, and to receive the grace of God as we enter into His Rest.
(See 2 Nephi 31:20).

Echoing the exhortations of Book of Mormon prophets, Abraham Lincoln declared on March 30, 1863, that "it is the duty of nations as well as of men and women to owe their dependence upon the over-ruling power of God, to confess their sins and transgressions in humble sorrow. Yet with assured hope that genuine repentance will lead to mercy and pardon, (we) recognize that those nations only are blessed whose God is the Lord." (See 1 Nephi 2:20).

When we commence a reading of The Book of Mormon for the first time, it would be well to remember that belief is a mental assent to the truth, without the moral element of responsibility that we call faith. To those to whom much is given, however, more is expected. The gift of faith requires action. Therefore, "faith without works is dead, being alone." (James 2:17).

"Jesus Christ (is) the Son of God, (and is) the Father of heaven and earth, the Creator of all things." (Mosiah 3:8). Reverently, we take His name upon ourselves, called by the name of Christ in a familial way. For 'he hath spiritually begotten (us)" taught Benjamin. (Mosiah 5:7). This singular family relationship is the reserve of the faithful, and it is in addition to the incontrovertible reality that every one of us is a spirit child, created by our Father in Heaven. It seems that, within the blueprint of the Plan, it has been preordained that the universe truly is a machine whose purpose is for the making of gods.

As they were immersed in the stream, righteous Nephites and Lamanites qualified for membership in the Lord's church, but that ordinance did not assure them of the spiritual transformation that was necessary to regain the presence of God. That came thru the baptism of fire and the Holy Ghost, for it was "by the water (that they kept) the commandment; by the Spirit (that they were) justified, and by the blood (of Jesus Christ) that they were (ultimately) sanctified." (Moses 6:60).

Missionaries who are of the caliber of the Sons of Mosiah are the agents of the Lord, and dispense the oil of gladness by bringing the knowledge of God to all those who harken to the good news. But more than that, those who've died without having had the opportunity to obtain such wisdom will yet be given an opportunity to receive and accept the gospel in their life after death, that they, too, might become heirs of the kingdom of God.

In the modern-day state of Israel, those who are known by the name 'Sabra' are the native born children of the Covenant. The fruit of the prickly pear cactus, the sabra, has a dry and unappealing skin. But inside, it is sweet, juicy, and is pleasing to the taste. Just so, when God measured the Nephites, He didn't look at their coarse exteriors, but on the inner vessels. His measuring tape went, not around their heads, but around their hearts.

As long as they
made consistent deposits
into what has been described
as a spiritual bank account, the
Nephites rarely found themselves
overdrawn during times of need.
In moments of crisis, the Savior
would call upon their bounteous
reserves to soothe their troubled
souls. With David, they could
cry out to the Savior: "Thou
anointest my head with
oil! My cup runneth
over!" (Psalms
23:5).

When we are having
discussions with investigators
who mirror the spiritual immaturity
of the poor Zoramites, we mustn't forget
that they need milk, and not meat, in order to
nourish their belief. Tender shoots that spring
from young testimonies need to be carefully
nurtured. Ecclesiastical embroidery often
unnecessarily complicates the stitchery
of the simple gospel messages that
we carry in our hearts, that we
wear on our coat sleeves,
and that come from
our lips.

Among the Nephites, the authority of the priesthood could only be exercised under the direction of the one holding the right, which was the key to its implementation. Its power only functioned in accordance with the characteristics and attributes of God; namely persuasion, long-suffering, gentleness, meekness, love unfeigned, righteousness and virtue, knowledge, justice, judgment, mercy, and truth. It ceased to exist when it was used to obtain the honors of the world, or to gratify pride, to cover up sins or evil, or to exercise unrighteous dominion.

Study, prayer, and our devotion empower us as they enlarge our souls and enlighten our understanding as we read The Book of Mormon. As Brigham Young famously said: "Every gospel principle carries within it a witness that it is true." From the matchless economy that is such a prominent characteristic of heaven, "we often catch a spark from the awakened memories of the immortal soul, which lights up our whole being as with the glory of our former home." (Joseph F. Smith).

For far too long, Israel has "drunk of the dregs of the cup of trembling." (2 Nephi 8:23). At last, she will put on her strength by exercising the authority of the Priesthood of God. As Moroni exhorted: "Awake, and arise from the dust, O Jerusalem; yea, and put on thy beautiful garments, O daughter of Zion; and strengthen thy stakes, and enlarge thy borders forever, that thou mayest no more be confounded, that the covenants of the Eternal Father which he hath made unto thee, O house of Israel, may be fulfilled." (Moroni 10:31).

The Lord has given us repeated reassurance that it is His hand that will rule in the Last Days, and so His people need not fear the vile threats and dreadful oaths of the wicked. He has promised: "I will make thy horn iron, and I will make thy hoofs brass. And thou shalt beat in pieces many people; and I will consecrate their gain unto the Lord, and their substance unto the Lord of the whole earth." (3 Nephi 20:19).

We
learn in
The Book of
Mormon that
we aren't born
born of blood, or
even of water, but
of spirit in celestial
realms, and thus we
trace the pattern of
a nobler heritage.
We are offspring
of God, born of
royalty and
bathed in
light.

The
Nephites were
never promised by
God that the sky would
always be blue, or that they
would walk along flower-strewn
paths all their lives thru. Nor did He
guarantee they would have sun without
rain, joy without sorrow, and peace without
pain. What He did promise was strength for
the day, rest from their labors, and light for
their way; grace for their trials, help from
above, unfailing sympathy, and most
importantly, His undying love."
(Anonymous).

The
Savior
employed
the metaphor
of the mote and the
beam to illustrate that
it seems to be our human
nature to point out the sins
of others, and emphasize their
weaknesses, although it is we
who are often the party that is
guilty of the more serious
transgression. (See
3 Nephi 14:2).

The
highest pinnacle
upon which the Nephites
hoped to enjoy spirituality
was not bathed in unbroken
sunshine, but in their absolute
and undoubting trust in the love of
God. They needed to endure a soaking
rain now and then, together with the mud
that followed the deluge. Lest we forget, the
Spirit was always there to remind them that
change often comes like a clap of thunder
and a flash of lightning. But after the
storm, flowers will bloom.

It was in the
best of times that white hot
sparks of faith were struck off
the divine anvil of God to ignite the
flames of resolve within the hearts of the
Nephites, and to energize their power to do
whatsoever was right. That kindled a fire
that would steadily burn as a bright
beacon of hope in anticipation of
the return of their God and
King in the latter
days.

The capable Pilot
guiding the Nephites
across uncharted waters as
they sailed the ocean of life is
our Lord and Savior Jesus Christ.
He never ceased to encourage them
to continually take their bearings on
eternity. They were reassured by brightly
burning stars that were ever twinkling over
a celestial horizon. Today, it may come at the
conclusion of a day trip or it may only be when
our life's voyage is over that we realize that the
wind and the waves are always on the side of
the ablest Navigator, Who as it turns out,
has all along been the Master and
Commander of our fragile
vessel on the far side
of the world.

A practical model for life is provided by our correct understanding of the principles and doctrine that forms the substance of The Book of Mormon. It allows us to reconcile our place in the cosmos with eternity, by giving us down to earth instruction relating to our heavenly potential. It gives us the tools to work out our salvation before the Lord, even as we deal with the distress of telestial trivia and grapple with the distractions of temporal trauma.

From the perspective of a broken heart and a contrite spirit, the psalmist wrote: "But as for me .. my clothing was sackcloth. I humbled my soul with fasting." (Psalms 35:13, see 2 Nephi 13:24). When the law is written upon our hearts, and we sense God's forgiveness, we must at that very moment seize the chance to forgive others, invoking spiritual powers that will bless our efforts, specifically because it is so contrary to our nature to do so. The god-like opportunity to forgive should never be wasted, because it can awaken within our hearts a spiritual sensitivity that is somehow greater than ourselves. On a related note, Brigham Young once told the Saints that "he who takes offense when none was intended is a fool, and he who takes offense when it was intended is usually a fool."

The Book of Mormon has
forged a link between the realities
of our physical world and the promises
of eternity. It has seamlessly harmonized
one with the other. It also provides us with
the practical tools we need to hash out the
details of our progression toward that
"undiscovered country from whose
bourn no traveler (will ever)
return." (Shakespeare,
"Hamlet," Act 3,
Scene 1).

The principle of opposition that is
repeatedly illustrated in Book of Mormon
stories clearly points to the Atonement as the only
reasonable alternative to an otherwise overwhelmingly
negative influence competing for dominance in our lives. It
stipulates that when we fall short of obedience to any of God's laws,
we travel the Royal Road of Repentance. This Requires that we act with
Responsibility, as we Recognize the Reality of our transgression and view
it with Revulsion and experience Remorse that drives us to our knees. In our
heart-felt prayers, we Relate to our Heavenly Father how we feel, in a process of
confession that is the most painful example of Revelation. This demands that
we Renounce our self-defeating behaviors, make Restitution where possible to
injured parties, and then do whatever is necessary, as the Spirit directs us,
to submit ourselves to a Refiner's fire that will help us to Re-establish a
Reconciliation with heaven and Regain the Rapport with Jesus Christ
that had formerly been our hope and our joy. As we Renew our
Resolve to Recommit ourselves to walk the covenant path, it
will be through the miracle of the grace of Him Who is
our Redeemer, that we will Receive a Remission of
our sin. Only then, will it become possible to
move forward with purpose toward our
Reward in heaven.

If the unequaled example of the
Sons of Mosiah (see Alma 17:2-3), has
taught us anything, it is that we must not
allow our prejudices to influence the depth of our
compassion, or allow debate to determine the merits of
the petitions of the impoverished before we decide whether it
is prudent to provide them with aid. Ammon, Aaron, Omner,
and Himni rightly ignored the protestations of their brethren
in Zarahemla who had characterized the wicked Lamanites to
whom they desired to minister as "a stiffnecked people, whose
hearts delight in the shedding of blood, whose days have
been spent in the grossest iniquity, whose ways have
been the ways of a transgressor from the
beginning." (Alma 26:23-25).

Were it not for the righteous influence of
our Savior Jesus Christ, to Whom we have been
benevolently reintroduced in The Book of Mormon,
"we wait for light, but behold obscurity; for brightness,
but we walk in darkness. We grope for the wall like the blind
... as if we had no eyes. We stumble at noonday as in the night.
We are in desolate places as dead men. We roar like bears, and
mourn sore like doves. We look for judgment, but there is
none; for salvation, but it is far off from us. For our
transgressions are multiplied before (God),
and our sins testify against us."
(Isaiah 59:9-12).

It is in The Book of Mormon
where we encounter the bold statement
that if we are born of God, it will be because
we have received His image in our countenances
in a process wherein we have experienced a mighty
change in our hearts. (See Alma 5:14 & 26). Only
then, through saving faith, will we be prepared to
appropriately exercise our agency to decisively
deal with the opposition that is integral to
the successful execution of "the Great
and Eternal Plan of Deliverance
from Death." (2 Nephi
11:5).

All those who read it
may be privileged to discover that there
is an ethereal light that streams forth from
the pages of The Book of Mormon to illuminate
the work of our Heavenly Father's hands. It will show
us the way we must go in order to dwell within the secure
fold of the Good Shepherd, Who is "a lamp unto (our) feet,
and a light unto (our) path." (Psalms 119:105). In the
same vein, we discover that "all things bright and
beautiful, all creatures great and small. All
things wise and wonderful, the Lord
God made them all." (Cecil
Francis Alexander).

Book of Mormon doctrine is the gold
standard for those who have previously identified with
the Pharisees or with the Sadducees, with Buddha, Confucius,
Guru Nanak, Zoroaster, or with gods of wood and stone. It also
usurps the monotheism of Islam and the Bahá'i, the pantheistic
theology of Hinduism, Shintoism, and Taoism, and Eastern
Orthodoxy, as well as secular humanism and irreligion. It
trumps Protestantism, Catholicism, fundamentalism,
and evangelical Christianity, as well as existential
nihilism, skepticism, relativism, subjectivism,
rationalism, and the political, economic, and
social ideologies of the self-referential
postmodern world.

Comforter is an appropriate name for the Holy Spirit
or the Holy Ghost (see Moroni 8:26), for He is the author
of acumen, the avatar of agency, the architect of aptitude, the
benefactor of blessings, the champion of committed Christians,
the craftsman of comfort, the designer of our discipleship, the
engineer of erudition, the guarantor of gifts, the initiator
of insight, the inventor of intelligence, the patron of
perception, the provider of praise, the sponsor
of scholarship, and the power that is
behind the upwelling of our
understanding.

We have seen repeatedly in The Book of Mormon how the Devil, when given an opportunity, will capitalize on our weakness by using subtlety, as he pacifies and lulls us into a counterfeit sense of carnal security, making us believe that we are gaining something when we are instead losing. He does this to quietly avoid awakening our faculties to harsh realities. He distorts our perspective by twisting our blessings inward so that they'll amplify our feelings of self-sufficiency. Such an emancipation from God, however, comes at the cost of an ironclad compact that is made with the author of sin.

Prophets of The Book of Mormon have repeatedly invited us to be baptized for "the remission of sins, (which) bringeth meekness, and lowliness of heart, and because of meekness and lowliness of heart cometh the visitation of the Holy Ghost, which Comforter filleth with hope and perfect love, which love endureth by diligence unto prayer, until the end shall come, when all the saints shall dwell with God."
(Moroni 8:26).

A dawn of recognition comes
when we study The Book of Mormon,
and in particular when we realize that we
are the "elect according to the foreknowledge
of God the Father, through sanctification of
the Spirit, unto obedience and sprinkling
of the blood of Jesus Christ." (1 Peter
1:2). We obtain "precious faith,"
and become partakers "of the
divine nature." (2 Peter
1:1 & 4).

A sometimes violent confrontation that occurs
between the principles and doctrines that are taught
in The Book of Mormon, on the one side, and the values
of society, on the other, tears at the fabric of our world. Our
efforts to remain true to God test the limits of our stability.
But in the process, we'll find new spiritual strength. When
we go the second mile by lengthening our stride, we burst
free of the shackles that had limited the expression of
our potential, and we receive the "gift of spiritual
independence that can remove the veil of
insensitivity to our destiny."
(Richard L. Gunn).

The Book of Mormon grounds us as we struggle to live in the world, while not falling into the snare of being of the world. Brigham Young has been purported to have said the following (but, alas, the quote has been categorically debunked online, in NothingWavering.org, on July 30, 2014, by J. Max Wilson): "The worst fear that I have about this people is that they will get rich, forget God, wax fat, kick themselves out of the church, and go to hell. They will stand mobbing, robbing, poverty, and all manner of persecution, and be true. But my greater fear for them is that they will not be able to stand wealth." Brother Brigham may not have said it, but it seems to make sense, and ring true, especially in light of Nephite history and of opulent residential construction in the neighborhoods surrounding the Draper, Utah temple.

It was decreed in heaven that every one of God's children would have exactly the same number of hours in a week, 168 to be exact, and much of it would be discretionary time to do with as they pleased. Every minute is sacred, but as few as two of these hours are spent in church, and not many more are typically devoted to scripture study. We need to ask ourselves: How many hours are wasted as we 'hang out,' or are squandered watching television, playing video games, or surfing the net on our computers, or on our mobile devices, or on social media?

The responsibility of the Holy
Ghost is to bear a sacred testimony of the
validity of every gospel ordinance. Because there
can be no greater witness than that of the Spirit, the
Atonement is activated in our behalf by the baptism of
fire and of the Holy Ghost. With that unimpeachable
witness, Mercy seals the deal that has been made
with Justice as the penitent faithful receive a
remission of their sins in a symbolic rite
of purification. (See 2 Nephi 31:17).

Those who have embraced
The Book of Mormon as holy scripture,
and have received the blessings that heaven "has
in store for the faithful, will be able to know the things
of God from the things which are not of Him, the light from
the darkness, that which comes from heaven, and that which
comes from somewhere else. This is the satisfaction and the
consolation that the Latter-day Saints enjoy by living
their religion. This is the knowledge which
everyone who thus lives possesses."
(Brigham Young).

The Apostle Peter
observed: "Of a truth, I perceive
that God is no respecter of persons.
But in every nation, he that feareth him,
and worketh righteousness, is accepted with
him." (Acts 10:34-35). When we receive The
Book of Mormon as holy scripture, we are
converted by the power of the Holy Ghost,
and we are carried along on the path
leading to eternal life.

In a beautiful admonition to the people of
Gideon, Alma described the qualities that we must
strive to emulate when we enter the waters of baptism. "Be
humble," he pleaded, "and be submissive and gentle; easy to be
entreated; full of patience and long-suffering; being temperate in
all things; being diligent in keeping the commandments of God
at all times; asking for whatsoever things ye stand in need, both
spiritual and temporal, always returning thanks unto God
for whatsoever things ye do receive. And see that ye have
faith, hope, and charity, and then will ye always
abound in good works." (Alma 7:23-24).

The mission of the Holy Ghost is to penetrate the exoskeletons of our rough exteriors to work on what He finds inside of us, namely our conscience, that He might then gently guide us beyond the first principles and ordinances of the gospel, onward and upward to covenants relating to the priesthood and the temple. "For behold, thus saith the Lord God: I will give unto the children of men line upon line, precept upon precept, here a little and there a little, and blessed are those who hearken unto my precepts, and lend an ear unto my counsel, for they shall learn wisdom, for unto him that receiveth, I will give more."
(2 Nephi 28:30).

It is the Light of Christ (see Moroni 7:16), that has been benevolently and universally bestowed upon all of us by One Whom we can be sure "denieth none that come unto him, black and white, bond and free, male and female; and he remembereth the heathen; and all are alike unto (Him), both Jew and Gentile." (2 Nephi 26:33). It stimulates soul-sweat as it works on our conscience, our sense of duty, and our scruples, in the face of relentless opposition in all things. (See 2 Nephi 2:11).

It is in
The Book of Mormon
where we learn how to "caress
the tender chords of associations, of
gratitude, loyalty, and appreciation, of
selflessness, helpfulness, and forgiveness, of
friendship, love, and compassion." It moves us,
with "truth discovered and accepted, of beauty
created and enjoyed, of goodness deepened
and made manifest in life."
(P.A. Anderson).

The Book of Mormon give us the tools to
circumvent religious roundabouts, to steer
clear of conceptual cul-de-sacs, and to avoid the
pitfalls of doctrinal dead-ends, so that we might
"come unto Christ, (and be) perfected in him, (to)
deny (ourselves) of all ungodliness; and if (we)
shall deny (our)selves of all ungodliness, and
love God with all (our) might, mind and
strength, then is his grace sufficient
for (us), that by his grace (we)
may be perfect in Christ."
(Moroni 10:32).

As we engage in a dialogue with our nonmember friends who are struggling to feel the influence of the Light of Christ as they make initial forays into The Book of Mormon, we mustn't pretend to know everything. We need to recognize if we've been "speed listening," or formulating retorts in our mind, when we should instead have been paying closer attention to what they have been saying. We need to resist the temptation to treat every conversation as if it were a debate, and we need to remember the wisdom of Isaiah, who counseled: "Come now, and let us reason together." (Isaiah 1:18).

The Book of Mormon blesses us with the capacity to squarely face even our most stubborn challenges. It helps us to be one with the Saints, even as we celebrate our individuality and diversity. It nurtures us to move from dependence, through independence, and finally to the mature state of interdependence. It gives us the tools to enjoy conformity without at the same time sacrificing what makes each of us unique.

The truth be told, many of our friends and neighbors are very close to receiving their own witnesses of the divine origin of The Book of Mormon. If they would just change one or two behaviors or beliefs, they would be spot-on. But here's a radical thought, though. What if, instead, we changed just one or two of our own behaviors, or we viewed our neighbors' beliefs in a more tolerant and ecumenical light? Might that not become a more powerful tool of conversion?

The Book of Mormon gives our spiritual muscles pliancy and flexibility, that there might be room for the companionship of the Holy Ghost, "which maketh manifest unto the children of men, according to their faith." (Jarom 1:4). We will always be subjected to the effects of adversity and opposition, but without the therapeutic benefits of Book of Mormon teachings, we may needlessly suffer from a stiff neck that prevents us from looking up to Heavenly Father for guidance, over to priesthood leaders for counsel, around to seek out those in need, and down in an attitude of humility.

The Last Days are a mirror of those of Mormon, who wrote that "the power of the evil one was wrought upon all the face of the land" because of the lack of faith of the people. (Mormon 1:19). The world desperately needs The Book of Mormon because, whether it is aware of it or not, it is the spiritual equivalent of the boost that we receive after consuming a power bar or energy drink 30 minutes before engaging in physical activity, or in combat with the Devil.

The Book of Mormon warns us against our succumbing to a politically correct tolerance that embraces all sorts of deviant behavior. There are flim-flam artists abroad in the land who seek to adroitly fleece us of our very identity as the children of God, and most of the time, we are not even aware that the theft is taking place. "Vice is a monster of such frightful mien, as to be hated needs but to be seen. Yet seen too oft, familiar with her face, we first endure, then pity, then embrace." (Alexander Pope). We have come full circle from Eve's temptation in the Garden of Eden. Once again, we are beguiled by the allure of tinkling cymbals and sounding brass (not to mention shiny red apples).

The Book of Mormon introduces us to a familiarity with principles that stands in sharp contrast to the values of society that are continually morphed by the shifting sands of cultural expediency. The covenant path that Book of Mormon prophets have encouraged us to follow will protect us from these mutating tenets, and it provides a stable moral basis during the process of our development into the full stature of our spirits.

The Book of Mormon teaches that our little ones are the nobility of heaven, and that they are members of a chosen generation with divine destinies. And so, we will make whatever sacrifices are necessary to ensure their success. They come to us from their heavenly home "like gentle rain thru darkened skies, with glory trailing from their feet as they go, and endless promise in their eyes." While under our care, they grow tall and strong, "like silver trees against the storm; who will not bend with the wind or the change, but stand to fight the world alone."
(Doug Stewart).

The Book of Mormon pointedly alludes to an age of accountability (see Moroni 8:4-26), suggesting that those who have reached the tender age of eight years find themselves so recently removed from the certainty and stability of the eternal world, that they are often impatient to recapture the peaceful security and quiet serenity of that more relaxed, familiar, and predictable environment to which they had become accustomed. Baptism gives them the opportunity to enjoy the best of both worlds; to live on the earth, facing challenges, difficulties and adversity, but still experience a heavenly peace that surpasses understanding.

Until our hearts have been broken by contrition, and we have acknowledged the power of our Father in Heaven by casting off the self-limiting conditions and the self-defeating behaviors that blind us to a larger view of life, we will never enjoy a settled conviction of the truth in our minds. The peace that follows our obedience to the celestial principles that are illuminated in The Book of Mormon brings a greater reality within our reach. When we realize that we are not alone, we will have begun a journey that will carry us to a higher state of being where we will find that we have been covered in star dust, as we mingle with the Gods. (See Genesis 3:22).

Surely, it must not be lost on our Savior Jesus Christ, Who after all, is the Creator of both heaven and earth, that water may be the most abundant compound to be found throughout His universe. (Hydrogen is by far its most abundant element. Oxygen, the third most abundant, likes to bind to hydrogen, and so water must be one of the most abundant molecules in the universe). It should not be lost on us that baptism by immersion in water for the remission of sins mut certainly be His universally recognized token of obedience to the principles of His gospel, worlds without end. There is no way for us to know this for sure, but it is probably the case throughout the cosmos. As those who wrote the Serek Scroll described it, the penitent are "for all the laws of God, and their flesh is cleansed, shining bright in the waters of purification, even in the waters of baptism. They shall be given a new name in due time to walk perfect in all His ways." ("The Serek Scroll," or "Manual of Discipline," was discovered in 1947, in caves high above Qumran. It dates from Book of Mormon times, to around 400 B.C.).

Those who've read The Book of Mormon may have experienced an epiphany reminiscent of that which was felt by Jeremiah, who wrote of the effect the scriptures had on him: "His word was in mine heart as a burning fire shut up in my bones, and I was weary with forbearing, and I could not stay." (Jeremiah 20:9). His description reminds us of the glory of celestial realms. "God Almighty Himself dwells in eternal fire. Flesh and blood cannot go there, for all corruption is devoured by that fire." (Joseph Smith).

When we give of ourselves, we create
an independence that can be exhilarating,
because it is accompanied by the recognition of
new-found and soul-expanding opportunities. It
crystalizes within us the realization that we are
spiritual beings having mortal experiences,
ennobling us with the sure knowledge
that only the powers of heaven can
countermand the dizzying
inequities of life.

Whenever we happen to
encounter a poor, wayfaring man of grief
who is down and out, an ounce of assistance will
always be better than a pound of preaching. Socrates
advised us: "Know thyself," and Cicero urged: "Control
Thyself," while in The Book of Mormon we are taught to
give of ourselves while memorializing our commitment
to actively embrace every demand of discipleship by
following the example of the Savior. After all, "are
we not all beggars? Do we not all depend upon
the same Being, even God, for all (of) the
substance which we have?" (Mosiah
4:19, see Alma 32:16).

*Reflection
can be positive, motivating, and
energizing when it is the Light of Christ
that is brightly shining upon our features. As
Alma asked the people of Zarahemla, "And now,
behold, I ask of you, my brethren of the church,
have ye spiritually been born of God? Have ye
received His image in your countenances?
Have ye experienced this mighty
change in your heart?"
(Alma 5:14).*

*With Enos, we "rejoice in
the day when (our) mortal shall
put on immortality, and (we) shall
stand before him. Then shall (we) see his
face with pleasure, and he will say unto
(us): Come unto me, ye blessed, there
is a place prepared for you in the
mansions of my Father."
(Enos 1:27).*

"For this end
was the (Book of Mormon)
given," to prepare us to be like the
Savior, until "we are made alive in
Christ, because of our faith."
(2 Nephi 25:25).

We mustn't postpone
until we are spiritually dead to the Light
of Christ the inevitability of the unremitting
invitation from the Holy Ghost to gain our own
Book of Mormon testimony. When we no longer
are able to make the vital distinction between
light and darkness, we risk becoming
subject to the wiles of that fallen
being who rules the night.
(See Alma 34:35).

The Spirit of the Lord
withdraws and Satan has power
over the children of men when they
willfully disparage The Book of Mormon
and lead the children of God astray. This is
the state of the unrepentant wicked, from which
there may be no recovery. When the sword of
Justice falls, it will be for them as if there
had been no redemption made, and the
power of the Atonement will be of
no effect. (See Alma 34:35
& 42:27-30).

The messages that have been woven
in to the epic themes of The Book of Mormon
are intended to change not only our behavior, but
also our nature. Perfect obedience to its principles and
doctrines qualifies us to enter into the Rest of the Lord.
The covenants that are described in the book have the
power to move us along the path of progression to
the point where we will internalize the divine
nature of God and will feel comfortable
in His holy presence.

Book of Mormon prophets have inquired of us if we'll be chaste in our behavior and if we will love others; if we will discipline our nature and be righteous stewards. They beg us to love our less fortunate brothers and sisters, to take proper care of our bodies, and to try to stay in touch with the Spirit, to better comprehend God's omniscience. They invite us to pray for an understanding of the gift of His Son, and to ponder the power of His Atonement by participating in the ordinances of the gospel and by entering into sacred covenants with Him.

As we investigate the significant themes that trace their way through The Book of Mormon, we begin to understand how our covenants with God help us to overcome adversity and gain self-mastery. We learn that covenants can help us to focus our efforts to become as He is. As we do so, it begins to dawn on us that this is the purpose of the covenants that we are invited to make with Him. With a quickening pulse, we begin to understand that it is our covenants that prepare us to become as God is, and to feel comfortable in His presence.

It should be
self-evident, but whenever
the Nephites trivialized celestial
sureties, they became more susceptible
to the enticements of the Devil. Without the
protective influence and guidance of the Holy
Ghost, they were vulnerable to the lethal storms
sweeping across the face of the earth which were
initiated by the destroyer. Then, as they lost
the ability to resist these telestial tempests,
the suffocating storms of Satan sucked
the very life-sustaining marrow from
their bones into the vortex of
oblivion.

Following the post-
mortal ministry of the Savior
among the Nephites in the land that
was round about Bountiful, the powers of
heaven and earth amplified each other, and
carried them along on the harmonic waves of
the Spirit. All their trappings and pretenses
were shorn away, outward observances and
phylacteries were stripped from the ritual
of their worship, until only their true
feelings remained to be quickened
by the gentle touch of the
Holy Ghost.

At the place of Mormon, raw and ugly sores that had been inflicted upon Alma's little flock by worldly influences back in the court of King Noah were healed in the waters of baptism. (See Mosiah Chapter 18). The Balm of Gilead prevailed over even the most powerfully persistent pestilences that were festering in Babylon.

Simply put, The Book of Mormon exposes us to the process by which we progress. Heavenly Father has given us the book in the Last Days to test our mettle. This is why having the courage to be true to our convictions is so intimately tied to gaining a testimony of that book of holy scripture. It is only when we've acted on the basis of faith that we will receive a spiritual confirmation of the power that continues to drive the Restoration forward, as our feelings of self-confidence grow and our tentative overtures are replaced by purposeful actions.

The relevancy
of King Benjamin's counsel to
his people in the land of Zarahemla and the
significance of the order in which it was given
is self-evident: "This much I can tell you," he said.
"If ye do not watch yourselves, and your thoughts,
and your words, and your deeds, and observe the
commandments of God, and continue in the
faith ... even unto the end of your lives,
ye must perish." (Mosiah 4:30).

There is a veritable groundswell of
emotion that is stimulated by the Light
of Christ. It generates the energy to carry us
heavenward in the direction of a testimony of
The Book of Mormon. Our devotion is elevated
to something more dynamic than the simple
mechanical observance of a multiplicity of
ceremonial rules. Seeking its guidance
as well as that of the Holy Ghost as we
study is the daily antidote to our
tendency toward selfishness,
pride, and self-reliance.

One of the problems that the Nephites repeatedly faced was that they often failed to generate the spiritual horsepower to express with action their feelings about the Savior. Such was the case when Jesus asked the Pharisees: "What think ye of Christ? Whose son is he?" (Matthew 22:41-42). Sadly, their sluggish response was tendered without affection or emotion. Its dearth of traction was obvious, its inability to generate spontaneity was palpable, its lack of energy to engage enthusiasm was noticeable, its incapacity to spark vitality was evident, and its failure to candidly acknowledge the powerful relationship that could have existed between themselves and God was indisputable.

The innocuous question posed by the Savior: "What think ye of Christ?" (see Matthew 22:42 & Alma 5:20) has always demanded of Pharisees, Nephites, and others, that they dig deeply within themselves as they have been invited to bear their witness, because it is all too easy to stammeringly retreat into colorless and insipid verbiage as the easy way out. No matter who we might be, if we casually or carelessly steer our course away from Him with offhand, dismissive, or inconsiderate comments, until He is conveniently out of sight and mind, we can realistically expect in return no more than a stupor of thought.

When we enthusiastically
embrace The Book of Mormon,
we unleash a spiritual cornucopia.
We partake of the nourishing bread of
life that has been provided, drink from a
well of living water, and with renewed
energy, we "lift up (our) heads and
receive the pleasing word of God,
and feast upon His love."
(Jacob 3:2).

Those who've accepted the
challenge of the missionaries to read, study,
and pray about The Book of Mormon with open
hearts and minds will stand out in sharp contrast to
undisciplined souls who've been seduced by the siren song
of Satan's sentinels. Without the stabilizing influence of the
Spirit, unprincipled character crumbles when faced with telestial
temptations that are tantalizing and yet so very traumatizing.
These treasures of the earth are worthless counterfeits of the
blessings that God has reserved for the faithful. It is this
substitution of the sacred by the profane that is an
abomination in the sight of God.

The Nephites' obedience
to the Law of the Sabbath introduced
them to a day of worship and of rest, that
they might find refuge far from the tumult of
the teeming multitudes of the maddingly telestial
crowd. Their observance protected them from choking
on their possessions, whose opacity might have otherwise
clouded their ability to experience illumination by the
Spirit. Focusing on the kingdom, especially on the
Sabbath day, helped them to differentiate between
wheat and tares, maintain their perspective,
and strengthen their reverence
for the work.

Too often, it seems that the Nephites
quite painfully recognized that they had
sought "all the days of (their) lives for that
which (they could not) obtain, and ... ha(d)
sought for happiness in doing iniquity,
which thing is contrary to the nature
of that righteousness which is in
our great and Eternal Head."
(Helaman 13:38).

The Book of Mormon provides valuable insight into the spiritual roots of our relationships that are the products of our interconnectivity and interdependence. These are essential if we want to live in the world without being tarnished by it. In the end, abundance will be "multiplied unto (all those who have taken the time and made the effort to study the scriptures) through the manifestations of the Spirit." (D&C 70:13). Righteous objectives stay in focus when we pay attention to the guideposts that have been so abundantly provided within the book. These mile markers help us to stay focused and remain on track during our perilous journey through mortality.

The Book of Mormon provides us with many illustrations of Nephites who lived "after the manner of happiness." (2 Nephi 5:27, also see Alma 41:11, Helaman 13:38, & 3 Nephi 27:11). This was possible only when their level of understanding and their behavior harmonized with celestial principles, and for as long as they could feel the Light of Christ and the influence of the Holy Ghost. They needed to constantly remind themselves that there could be no discrepancy between their moral behavior and foundation gospel parameters. They knew that a deviant lifestyle, when short-lived pleasure in worldly ways was strangled by sin, couldn't be maintained, learning by the school of hard knocks and by sad experience that whenever they came away from mischief and found themselves fighting for air, it was because, at the end of the day, their "wickedness never was happiness." (Alma 41:10).

For millions of Latter-day Saints, The Book of Mormon has become a divinely inspired portal to the principles, ordinances, and covenants that enable them to be sanctified, to one day be worthy to live once again in a state of holiness in the presence of God. By following its teachings, all may come unto Christ, and lay hold upon every good gift … and be perfected in him, (as they) deny (themselves) all ungodliness." (Moroni 10:30 & 32). It is because of that book that all 8 billion of Heavenly Father's children who now dwell upon the earth may yet "continue in the supplicating of his grace" to one day stand blameless before Him at His Pleasing Bar.
(See Alma 7:3).

When we stand in holy places, and we are liberated from the cares and concerns of the world, the realities of eternity will illuminate our minds. As we read The Book of Mormon, if we listen very carefully, we will hear the gentle sound of the rustling of the robes of angels coming from behind a slightly-parted veil. The company of heavenly beings from the unseen world will sweep the cobwebs from our minds and open up to our unobstructed view undreamed vistas of otherwise inaccessible experience.

As we read, study, and pray about The Book of Mormon, we are invited to consider the possibility that we might in a coming day be like our Savior Jesus Christ because of His Atonement. We believe that His grace consists of the gifts and power by which we may be brought to His perfection and stature, so that we may enjoy not only what He has, but also what He is. We believe in the promise: "If ye by the grace of God are perfect in Christ, and deny not his power, then are ye sanctified in Christ by the grace of God, through the shedding of the blood of Christ, which is in the covenant of the Father unto the remission of your sins, that ye become holy, without spot." (Moroni 10:33).

Those who undertake a prayerful investigation of the merits of The Book of Mormon will very quickly see that it is not prejudicial. It doesn't play favorites nor does it pick sides. It simply levels the playing field for all of Heavenly Father's children. He knows that His Merciful Plan has enough wiggle room to allow our agency to find expression in myriad ways. The principles and doctrines found within its pages will always stand ready to guide us to a testimony of Jesus Christ, but in the meantime, we remain free to worship Almighty God according to the dictates of our own conscience. The "Author of Eternal Salvation" allows us to worship how, where, or what we may. (Hebrews 5:9, see also the Eleventh Article of Faith).

Our hope in Jesus Christ
(see Moroni 7:3), is buttressed by
the foundation scriptures of The Book of
Mormon. Our desire to believe is not wishful
thinking, nor is it misguided trust in promises
that cannot be fulfilled, and it is not a high-stakes
gamble that is based upon statistical improbabilities.
It is the inevitable reward of well-founded faith, when
we have developed the discipline to completely control
powerful thrusts within us, and to channel them
in the direction of testimony, to make sure our
priorities and desires remain in harmony
with gospel principles.

If we allow its magic to soften and change
our hearts, The Book of Mormon can become a
catalyst that propels us upward toward the discovery
of personal levels of experience with the Savior, for when
scripture speaks of "knowing Him," it must be referring
to a very special sense of the word. It is not enough that we
know about Him by reading the Gospels of Matthew, Mark,
Luke, and John, or by listening to others speak of Him. We
must know Him through the bonds of shared experience
and common feeling. In this way, our familiarity
with the book, which is a Second Witness of
Jesus Christ, becomes an immersion in
the tangible element of Spirit.

The Book of Mormon is as much involved with recovery as it is with discovery. Its objective is not union, but reunion with divine realities. The religious recognition that we experience when reading the book is a re-learning of what we have previously known. It is in this context that the word 'religion' may derive from the Latin root 'ligare' – 'to bind.' Thus 'religion' would mean 'to bind again.' This fits nicely with the perspective that links religion to a reunion or a reconnection with a divine purpose or, as some would say, with a Plan of Salvation for the children of our Heavenly Father.

The prophets of The Book of Mormon invite us over and over again to do more than make resolutions that, too often, are nothing more than empty promises to ourselves that are generally kept for only a few days or weeks at best, before they are abandoned and we return to our previously held behaviors. The book's emphatic presentation of principles and doctrine has staying power. It has no bias; its basis is belief that has been nurtured by a rich culture medium infused with the agar of faith, repentance, the ordinances of the gospel, covenants, and the Spirit. (See the Fourth Article of Faith).

Following their
exciting introduction to The Book
of Mormon, those who are investigating
"the merits, and mercy, and grace of the Holy
Messiah" (2 Nephi 2:8), have feelings that cannot
be formed into words. Suffice to say, that by the grace
of God, their eyes have been opened. The Savior has become
their Traveling Companion and trusted Advisor. He will help
them to forget their bad days and to become better by turning
lemons into lemonade; to love their families, and to be more
responsible and caring towards others. In short, to sacrifice
themselves through their love of all things bright and
beautiful, and all creatures great and small.

In the months following the
publication of The Book of Mormon,
gone were the days when those who had been
earnestly seeking the truth could remain content
to build upon the sepulchres of the fathers. No longer
would they be satisfied by reading histories, biographies,
and criticisms relating to the mission of the Savior and His
gospel. Third-person accounts would no longer suffice. All of
a sudden, The Book of Mormon stood as a testament that it
was now possible to individually and institutionally
tap directly into flowing fountains of living water,
to have a functioning, ongoing relationship
and companionship with the Spirit,
and with the Lord Himself.

The Greatest Story Ever Told is an appellation that has been ascribed, not only to the Bible, but now to The Book of Mormon. Both scriptures are meant to be signs and wonders to an unbelieving world. The Book of Mormon, in particular, was written to provide guidance to true believers in the Last Days. It is a story for good times as well as for hard times. It has the power to dismiss from our lives those worldly influences that always seem to be in competition with the issues of real substance, for example, that the heavens are open, and that revelation once again flows from a fountain of living water.

With The Book of Mormon, each of us has been fitted with a shield of faith that has been tailored to our unique needs. Its elements are strengthened by covenants that we make with Heavenly Father, that form the foundation of the book. We've made these individually, and not collectively, and we review and renew them repetitively. This protects us from getting caught up in the mechanics of the church, from killing the articles of its faith, and from permitting form to triumph over spirit. The kingdom is built by something as simple as our ardor and conviction, as we consciously nurture our relationship with God in a process that is informally initiated when we gain testimony of The Book of Mormon, and that legally and lawfully begins with our subsequent covenant of baptism by immersion for the remission of our sins.

By its very nature, the very existence of The Book of Mormon has contributed to "a great division among the people." (2 Nephi 30:10). In the Last Days, its adversaries are jockeying for position to control our minds, just as they did during our pre-mortal lives. Combatants with increasingly polarized ideologies have signed up to join a battle that has already commenced. (See Revelation 16:14).

Those who have prayed about The Book of Mormon when reading it will often testify that it has compelled them to internalize gospel principles. It teaches them to view their lives from an eternal perspective, which makes it easier to discern the polarized opposites that are so prevalent in our society today. When we see through the clarifying lens of faith, we can more easily distinguish happiness from its worldly counterfeits, such as pleasure, desire, decadence, sensuality, gratification, indulgence, carnality, and amusement. The Book of Mormon makes it possible, when we are weighed in the balances after living in the world, to be quickened by the Spirit (See Daniel 5:27).

When we find a quiet place to sit down with The Book of Mormon because we have determined to seriously read, study, and pray about its messages, our religious awareness will be mystically transformed by faith into a re-cognition and a re-knowing, while its principles and its doctrine will be re-entrenched as the sum and substance of our existence. The Holy Ghost will help us to deal with a telestial inclination to suppress that instinctive response. If, in any way, we initiate attempts to thwart the intrinsic Light of Christ, we will be "accountable, and to a degree, we will condemn ourselves. We knew Christ before this life, we know Him now and we will know Him hereafter. His sheep do indeed know His voice." (Truman Madsen).

Every now and then during our inquiry, we will confront a Doubting Thomas who demands physical proof relating to The Book of Mormon as a condition of their belief. They seek to circumvent the process by which faith and knowledge are developed. They demand evidence but refuse to pay the price. As with the adulterer, they seek the result but are unwilling to accept the responsibility.

The Prophet Joseph recorded in his History that an angel had told him that the book that was hidden in the Hill Cumorah was written upon gold plates. (See J.S.H. 1:34). However, The Book of Mormon record itself doesn't corroborate the Angel Moroni's characterization of the golden composition of the plates. In the church, however, it is commonly accepted that the records, other than the Plates of Brass, were 'plates of gold.'

The Three Witnesses to The Book of Mormon wrote that they had "seen the plates which contain this record" without referencing the specific composition of the metal, although they went into great detail to describe the engravings themselves and their purpose to benefit humanity. Various Book of Mormon record-keepers referred to "plates of ore." "Plates of gold" are mentioned only twice, in Mosiah 8:9 and 28:11, where they specifically refer to the 24 Gold Plates of Ether. Mormon, who had access to all the records, and who personally abridged many of them, never referred in his writings to plates of gold, other than in these two references in the Book of Mosiah.

We really don't know how many, if any, of the plates from which Joseph Smith translated the record were actually made of gold, but we know they were heavy. The Eight Witnesses to The Book of Mormon testified that the plates they were shown and "hefted" had "the appearance of gold." The bound plates they handled are estimated to have weighed in the neighborhood of 80 pounds. The plates from which Joseph translated The Book of Mormon may have been thin sheets of gold, but the text itself suggests that, in general, Nephite prophets laboriously engraved their records on a variety of metals.

Because the element of gold itself seems to have been plentiful in the lands of The Book of Mormon, it many have not mattered to the Nephites of what material the plates were crafted. Jacob reported that his people, who still had an 'Old World' mindset, had "begun to search for gold, and for silver, and for all manner of precious ores, in the which, this land ... doth abound most plentifully." (Jacob 2:12). In the same vein (no pun intended), Mormon reported: "Both the Lamanites and the Nephites ... did have an exceeding plenty of gold, and of silver, and of all manner of precious metals." (Helaman 6:9).

Mormon's son twice referred to the plates, but only in reference to hiding them in the earth. (See Ether 15:11, & Mormon 8:4). Likewise, "Ammaron, being constrained by the Holy Ghost, did hide up the records which were sacred, yea, even all the sacred records which had been handed down from generation to generation, which were sacred." (4 Nephi 1:48-49).

It may simply be that the custodians of the records from which The Book of Mormon was translated were more focused on their messages than they were on the materials upon which they had been engraved.

In what could be traced to the very instant when their unsatisfied craving for the praise and the popularity of the world began to sway their behavior, the Nephites found themselves in the uncomfortable position of bending their character, when they thought they were only taking a bow. It was chiefly at this time that they needed the soothing inspiration of the Holy Spirit, and the healing guidance of their Lord and Savior Jesus Christ, and finally the nurturing encouragement of their Father, Who looked down upon them every day of their lives from heaven above.

It is the gospel of Jesus Christ as it is revealed in The Book of Mormon that encourages us to be enthusiastic. After all, it is the good news that practically begs us to experience the feeling of being possessed by a god, to have supernatural inspiration, and enjoy prophetic frenzy. This definition found in the dictionary is unmistakable. If we are suffused with enthusiasm, our actions are no longer ours; for it is God Who has taken control of our destiny, with kindness and benevolence.

"The version of Isaiah that is found in the Nephite scriptures hews an independent course for itself, as might be expected of a truly ancient and authentic record. It makes additions to the present text in certain places, omits material in others, transposes, makes grammatical changes, finds support at times for its unusual readings in the ancient Greek, Syriac, and Latin Versions, and at other times finds no support at all. In general, it presents phenomena of great interest to the student of Isaiah."
(Sydney B. Sperry).

"The text of Isaiah in The Book of Mormon is not word for word the same as that of the King James Translation. Of 433 verses of Isaiah in the Nephite record, Joseph Smith modified 234, or 53%. Some of the changes were slight, while others were radical. However, 199 verses are word for word the same as the K.J.T. We, therefore, freely admit that Joseph Smith may have used the K.J.T. when he came to the text of Isaiah on the plates. As long as the K.J.T. agreed substantially with the text on the plates, he let it pass; when it differed too radically, he translated the Nephite version and dictated the necessary changes."
(Sydney B. Sperry).

Early-on in the text of The Book of Mormon, we discover a verse that explains why a comprehension of Isaiah is so difficult, even for biblical scholars. Nephi said: I "speak somewhat concerning the words which I have written, which have been spoken by the mouth of Isaiah. For behold, Isaiah spake many things which were hard for many of my people to understand; for they know not concerning the manner of prophesying among the Jews." (2 Nephi 25:1). That is to say, the prophet Isaiah spoke in figures, using types and shadows to illustrate his points. Thus, the key to an understanding of his scriptural code requires some elucidation.

Among the Nephites, only Sam and Nephi, and perhaps their wives, had lived 'at Jerusalem.' Therefore, they alone had a first-hand understanding of their cultural heritage and the distinctive writing style of the Jews. On the one hand, it would be important that the righteous descendants of Lehi be familiar with the contents of the Plates of Brass, because their teachings from that body of scripture included many important doctrinal truths. On the other hand, Nephi abhorred that part of the Jewish mindset which had been responsible for his family's persecution, its expulsion from their home in the land of Jerusalem, their trials in the wilderness, and the hardship of their lives on the sea, and later in the land of promise.

The 'Isaiah Chapters' may have been strategically placed within the Second Book of Nephi in order to give first-time readers of The Book of Mormon time to acquaint themselves with the "manner of the Jews" (2 Nephi 25:2), through a study of the 22 chapters of the First Book of Nephi, and the first 11 chapters of the Second Book of Nephi, so that when they finally got to 2 Nephi Chapter 12, they could better appreciate the prophet's style and subject matter. Rather than summarily skipping over these chapters, Nephi might have hoped that, with their providential placement, latter-day Israel would be in a better position to understand Isaiah's messages, for both he and the resurrected Lord felt that his words were of great worth. (See 3 Nephi 23:1).

Only when we have expended soul-sweat, not only while studying 2 Nephi Chapters 12 to 24, but also while earning a familiarity with 1 Nephi Chapters 1-22, and 2 Nephi Chapters 1-11, will the words of Isaiah flow more easily and poetically to our minds. Scriptural fluency will come after practice that is manifested by memorization, recitation, individual and cooperative study, comparison with Isaiah's companion scriptures, and expansion of understanding by critical analysis of supportive commentaries, not to mention enduring faith, fervent prayer, and the illumination of our minds by the Spirit.

"Ye ought to search these things. Yea, a commandment I give unto you, that ye search these things diligently; for great are the words of Isaiah. For surely he spake as touching all things concerning my people which are of the house of Israel; therefore, it must needs be that he must speak also to the Gentiles. And all things that he spake have been and shall be, even according to the words which he spake." (3 Nephi 23:1-4).

"Wherefore, hearken, O my people, which are of the house of Israel," wrote Nephi, "and give ear unto my words; for because the words of Isaiah are not plain unto you, nevertheless they are plain unto all those that are filled with the spirit of prophecy … Yea, and my soul delighteth in the words of Isaiah, for I came out from Jerusalem, and mine eyes hath beheld the things of the Jews, and I know that the Jews do understand the things of the prophets, and there is none other people that understand the things which were spoken unto the Jews like unto them, save it be that they are taught after the manner of the things of the Jews." (2 Nephi 25:4-6).

The Book of Mormon
asks us to take calculated and
acceptable risks, in order to break
free from the comfort zones, safety
nets, and ports of refuge to which the
timid apprehensively retreat at the first
sign of danger, to squeak out their lives
as they scurry about from one shadowy
sanctuary to another, in a flight from
both freedom and faith.

It is
our faith that
points us in the
direction of doctrine,
that when we encounter
the principles of the Plan
in The Book of Mormon, we
might all experience religious
recognition, or a re-knowing
of things we have previously
been taught. We will respond
to the truth with action that
has the form and substance
of a godly walk which is
a bold testament of our
confidence in God's
power to save.

"The English translation of the Hebrew word "wayehi" (often used to link two ideas or events), "and it came to pass," appears some 727 times in the King James Version of the Old Testament. The expression is rarely found in Hebrew poetic, literary, or prophetic writings. Most often, it appears in Old Testament narratives, such as the books by Moses that recounted the history of the children of Israel. As in the Old Testament, the expression in The Book of Mormon (where it appears some 1,404 times) occurs only in the narrative sections, and is conspicuously missing from its more literary miscellanies.

It is quite likely that Joseph Smith would not have used the phrase "and it came to pass" in his translation of the plates, or at least not consistently, had he created the record himself. Thus, the discriminating use of this Hebraic phrase in The Book of Mormon is further evidence that it is what it says it is – an inspired translation from reformed Egyptian with ties to the Hebrew language. (See Mormon 9:32-33).

As we continue our religious education, The Book of Mormon will help us to expand our spiritual capacity, and to see as God sees, and to know and understand as He does. When we turn our attention to the interesting phrase "and thus we see," that is used by the prophets, and to its related variants, we open our minds to pearls of great price and hidden treasures of knowledge.

But what about the cultural and literary milieu in which Joseph found himself as he translated the plates? By the 1820s, the classical distinctions relating to the use of the word "behold" had become blurred. In the 1828 edition of Webster's Dictionary, "the word "behold" was defined as: "to fix the eyes upon; to see with attention; to observe with care." In other words, the 19th Century definition focused only on directing one's attention to a particular event or person, while ignoring the other definitions that had been classically related to the introduction of new truth, and to dramatization of existing truth. But, as one might expect from the inspired translation of an ancient text, in The Book of Mormon, the word "behold" is true to the pattern of the ancient Hebrew Bible, rather than to its contemporary 1828 definition.

The prophets who wrote in, or are quoted in, The Book of Mormon point us to doctrine, and so it is that when we encounter within its pages vernacular that is so characteristic of ancient Hebraic patterns, we respond to the truth with actions that have both the form and the substance of a godly walk, and that testify of our faith in the divine origin of the plates and in their translation by the gift and power of God.

The truth freed the Nephites from sin, guilt, confusion, skepticism, apprehension, misgiving, uncertainty, and ignorance. It liberated them to make thoughtful choices, receive priesthood ordinances, and to serve others with more charity, influence, and significance. As they more fully enjoyed the blessings of the Plan of Salvation, continuing obedience to gospel principles moved them steadily forward along the path that leads back to our heavenly home and to the warm embrace of God.

Book of
Mormon
contraries
bless us with
the perspective
to see adversity
as diamond dust
that polishes us to a
high luster, and not
as the abrasive that
wears us down and
grinds us up.

The Book of
Mormon allows us to
be engaged and energized
as we journey through Babylon
at an unhurried and yet productive
pace. It captivates us by its simplicity,
but at the same time, we are immersed in
its intricacies, riveted by its rewards, and
wrapped up in its wonders. It patiently
anticipates our acknowledgement of
its ability to transform our lives
and guide us to the gates of
heaven, and it only waits
upon our initiative,
to do so.

The Book
of Mormon
endows us with
the strength to watch
ourselves judiciously, to
be the meticulous guardians
of our thoughts, the scrupulous
custodians of our words, and the
prudent caretakers of our deeds, to
fastidiously observe all of the
commandments of God by
continuing evenly in
the faith.

Nephi encouraged
us to put on the armour
of God, and to press forward
with resolution and steadfastness,
confidence, and a firm determination
in Christ, with a perfect brightness of hope,
or perfect faith, and charity, or a love of God
and of all men. When we do not just casually
sample the words of Christ as if we were pawing
through a box of chocolates, but feast upon them,
as if we were at a gathering of royalty, enduring
in righteousness through this veil of tears to the
very end, we will have eternal life, which is the
greatest of the gifts that may be bestowed on
us by our loving Heavenly Father.

We can be
fully converted to
the gospel, and even
have a testimony of The
Book of Mormon, but still
enjoy very special moments
of reconfirmation. The Spirit
sometimes works so powerfully
upon us that we can say that our
hearts have been changed through
faith on the name of Christ, that
we have been born of Him, and
that we have become His sons
and daughters, no longer to
have the disposition to do
evil or be mischievous,
but rather to do good
continually.

We are
converted to
the doctrine of
Christ in 2 Nephi
Chapter 31, as it calls
to us, bidding us to come
in out of the cold; out of the
darkness and into the light of
day. We are the acorns of mighty
oaks. Our testimonies of Christ will
inspire us to rediscover our link to
heaven, and to reconnect with our
intrinsic nobility, even as we
continue to blossom where
we have been planted.

The Book of Mormon illustrates that even the righteous do not become perfect overnight. Therefore, the Lord has promised that as often as we repent, He will forgive us our trespasses. He will give us enough rope to either hang ourselves or to lasso the stars and hitch our wagons to eternity. The choice is ours to make.

Faith, light, and truth may be recognized as irreducible common denominators. They are the essential elements of an equation that describes the foundation upon which a testimony of The Book of Mormon is created. "One for all, and all for one!" was the motto of the Three Musketeers. Without faith, light, and truth, said Joseph Smith, we would "degenerate from God, descend to the devil, and lose knowledge," and without it, we cannot become converted to the gospel.

If we remain courageously true to our moral compass, we won't jostle with others for the best seat in economy on the temptation train to hell. Elder Neal A. Maxwell said: "If we pause at every spur on the road, and explore every detour from the strait and narrow path, to get our ticket punched, as it were, by every uninformed skeptic whose personal agenda includes matters that we would normally dismiss as trivial, we risk weakening our faith" in The Book of Mormon's foundation principles.

Christianity enjoys prominence as the most universally recognized religion in history, comprising a majority of the population in 2/3 of the world's 196 countries. Almost 2 billion people, 31% of the world's citizens, claim membership in 33,820 identifiable denominations. Islam follows with 1.2 billion people, and there are 14 million Jews. (Source: World Christian Encyclopedia). The purpose of The Book of Mormon is not to detract from the devotion to correct principles of any Christian or non-Christian among whom they teach and testify. Those who are receptive to the messages of the Restoration are encouraged to keep what the Spirit has already taught them to be true. The only purpose of proselytizing is so that "faith might also increase in the earth, and that the Lord's everlasting covenant might be established." (D&C 1:21-22).

Certainly, our finest hours are those when our unexpected challenges have been met with extraordinary efforts. As did the Seven Dwarfs, when we embrace the tenets of The Book of Mormon, we whistle while we work out our salvation, because of the Atonement's miracle. We discover how our Heavenly Father has linked our own efforts to those of His Son. Happiness, as it turns out, is the object and the design of our existence, and will be the end thereof, if we follow the pathway of repentance that leads to it.

The legions of angels from heaven who have ministered on the earth in the Last Days for the benefit of the children of God have included Moroni and John the Baptist, as well and Peter, James, and John. As messengers of Jesus Christ, they have restored true doctrine. Because of the ministry of these and other servants, a prophet of God has been able to declare with confidence that "no power on earth or hell can overthrow or defeat that which God has decreed. Every plan of the adversary will fail; for the Lord knows the secret thoughts of men, and sees the future with a vision clear and perfect, even as though it were in the past." (Joseph Fielding Smith, Jr.).

Over and over, The Book of Mormon's prophets emphasized that the hazmat protocol of repentance was written into God's Plan to detoxify us from the cares and habituating influences of the world, as well as from the homogenization process that occurs as we are worn down by the vicissitudes of life.

The Book of Mormon shows us precisely how to be repeatedly re-vitalized, as we are re-introduced to a Magical Kingdom in which our hopes and our dreams really will come true, if only we will muster the faith to wish upon the star that one cold winter night so long ago twinkled over a manger near Bethlehem.

If we are startled by the corruptible reflection that stares back at us as we pass by the window of a great and spacious building (see 1 Nephi 8:31 & 11:36), we'll need to repent without hesitation, remembering that "the Lord seeth not as man seeth; for man looketh on the outward appearance, but the Lord looketh on the heart." (1 Samuel 16:7).

What about those of us who are not so sure of ourselves? What happens if we look in the mirror and see only the face of a stranger staring back at us? What if our knees wobble at the prospect of the leap of faith required as we tackle The Book of Mormon, including the Isaiah Chapters of Second Nephi? We are comforted by the way the Savior quiets our fears, as He gently whispers: "Be still, and know that I am God."

As our faith in the divine
origin of The Book of Mormon intensifies,
the Lord's glory will rest upon us. Principles and
doctrine will be revealed in marvelous simplicity and in
plainness. As we earnestly seek heavenly guidance, we
will experience the manifestation of power as angels
watch over us, directing and protecting us. We will
be blessed to witness the kingdom of God rolling
forth, even as the walls of Babylon's lies and
deceptions crumble and fall all about us.
Oases will spring up in the desert
and living water will slake
our thirst for truth.

When we've nurtured
a relationship with the Holy
Ghost, He becomes our mentor and
our teacher. If we are good students,
and have done our homework, He will
reward us with an illumination of the
truthfulness of The Book of Mormon
that will bathe our minds and our
spirits in a cascading current of
insight, intuition, inspiration
and revelation. Well ahead of
time, He will provide us with
the answer key to the exam
that will follow shortly on
the heels of the classes
that are part of our
curriculum in
mortality.

Until it
has embraced The
Book of Mormon, our
society will remain on the
fast-track to self-destruction.
As we've learned from D&C 1:16,
it seeks "not the Lord, to establish
his righteousness, but every man
walketh in his own way and after
the image of his own god, whose
image is in the likeness of the
world, and whose substance is
that of an idol which waxeth
old and shall perish in
Babylon ..... which
shall fall."

There is a nearly
impenetrable veil that
has been drawn across our
minds. But we have The Book
of Mormon and the unimpeachable
witness of the Holy Ghost to assist us
in our efforts to probe that mysterious
curtain. In the interim, many of us are
swayed by the siren song of Satan, and
are drawn to the treacherous shoals of his
spiritual instability, thereon to founder,
and to be pulled down by the riptides of
religious relativism or the undertow of
agnosticism, faithless skepticism,
or outright atheism.

If the Nephite
warriors from Captain
Moroni's time had allowed
themselves to succumb to fear,
and had permitted faithlessness to
hobble the expression of their actions,
what would have been left in the end
would have seemed a monochromatic
and one-dimensional compromise
leaving them with a hollow core
of emptiness in the pit of their
stomachs and terror in their
hearts. Faith, after all, is
fear that has said
its prayers.

It's when we read The
Book of Mormon that we will
feel the gentle caress of the hands
of the Master Potter, as He turns our
lives on the wheel of time. As the Artisan
of our destiny, we'll give Him permission to
mold us and shape us. (See Jeremiah 18:6). We
are the clay, and He is our potter; we are the work
of His hands. (See Isaiah 64:8). As our thoughts
turn to the Savior, we remain as impressionable
and pliable vessels to the things of the Spirit,
even though we may feel that we have been
previously fired in the white-hot
crucible of adversity.

The effort that we've put into making
the teachings of The Book of Mormon a part
of our lives will leave the world a better place than
when we found it. When we pass beyond the veil, we
will leave our loved ones with a legacy of both tangible
and undefinable remembrance. We will leave them with
testimony. We will leave them with gratitude for the
privilege and blessing to have been knit together
as families that are both the corporeal footing
and the ethereal foundation of Heavenly
Father's "Great Plan of Happiness."
(Alma 42:8).

The Book
of Mormon will
safeguard us from
spiritual identity theft.
Of the fact that we have a
Father in Heaven, there can be
no question, for "the Spirit itself
beareth witness with our spirit, that
we are the children of God." (Romans
8:16). We know this intuitively, as do
Primary children as young as three
years of age who sing the songs of
Zion that publish the truth that
every one of them is a child
of God.

Every time we pause
in our busy lives to engage The
Book of Mormon, we are overcome with
enthusiasm, virtue garnishes our thoughts,
and our confidence waxes strong. The doctrine of the
priesthood distils upon our head as the dews from heaven,
the Holy Ghost is our constant companion, and the power to
reach our goals flows without compulsory means. We experience
spiritual delight, without the rush of sensory overstimulation that
is so prevalent in our technological world. As fire in the sky, the air
in our theater of life is charged with an electricity representing the
inevitable merger of the universal encouragement of the Light of
Christ with the pointed and providential guidance that is
provided by the Spirit. (See Moroni 10:5).

Often, when we repent,
the Spirit will compel us to
jump from the frying pan right
into the fire. With practice, however,
when we make that leap of faith, we will
land on springboards to action. These will
vault us upward toward safety, where we will
confidently balance on pinnacles of perfection
that have been strategically positioned here
and there throughout the pages of The
Book of Mormon.

We read The
Book of Mormon
to obtain a testimony
of the divinity of the work,
and to be liberated from fear,
uncertainty, the apprehension
of danger, religious turmoil,
and from the vagaries of
conspiring men and
women in the last
days.

The Book
of Mormon will
plot a safe passage
through the minefields
of mortality. It documents
potential perils and pitfalls,
charts the recommended route
that leads to refuge, maps out
the success strategies to which
we need to adhere if we desire
to live abundantly, and
measures our progress
on the pathway to
perfection.

Nothing can make up for the dogged discipline that remains a prominent feature of our Book of Mormon scholarship. Cheap thrills will never replace its lofty rewards, and novelty and spectacle will not defeat, but only delay, implementation of its principles. The all-embracing influence of the Light of Christ inspires us to set our sights on the brightly burning beacon of the Holy Ghost, Who waits upon our initiative to guide us across a vast ocean of light toward the discovery of a new world.

It's been observed that fools rush in where angels fear to tread. It has always been a favorite strategy of the Devil to lead the imprudent into profligate and improvident behavior with a flaxen cord around their necks that, initially, might actually feel quite comfortable. (See 2 Nephi 26:22). But once habit patterns have become firmly entrenched, the imprudent may be unpleasantly surprised to discover that they have sacrificed their agency to act independently, as they are bound under the yoke of sin by new routines that have taken hold and that are very difficult to change. Thus, does the Devil seek to bind us with his strong chains.

Opposition
can be a powerful force
that constantly refines us
as it pushes, pulls, and tears
away at us within the crucible of
experience. On our own, we cannot
eliminate the consequences of sin,
which, unfortunately, is often the
companion of opposition. For that
to happen, The Book of Mormon
re-introduces us to the Lamb
of God Who was slain from
the foundation of the
world.

Prophets in The Book
of Mormon encourage us to
inaugurate relationships with
Jesus Christ that are founded
on covenants, to stand beside
Him, and to weigh in on His
side of the scale, even as the
counterfeit coin of Satan's
spurious currency clatters
down in a cacophony of
confusion on the other
side of the scale.

The Book of
Mormon repeatedly illustrates
how our baptism is accompanied by "the
remission of sins (which) bringeth meekness,
and lowliness of heart; and because of meekness
and lowliness of heart cometh the visitation of the
Holy Ghost, which Comforter filleth with hope
and perfect love, which love endureth by
diligence unto prayer, until the end
shall come, when all the saints
shall dwell with God."
(Moroni 8:26).

The most
important thing when reading,
studying, and praying about The Book
of Mormon is to nurture the faith to believe it
came forth by the gift and power of God and that "as
(our) Lord and (our) God liveth it is true." (D&C 17:6).
He Who was ultimately responsible for the safe keeping of
the records declared: "Behold I am Moroni, and were it possible,
I would make all things known unto you." (Mormon 8:12). In a
coming day, we'll have the opportunity to ask him how he was able to
pull off such a feat, for he wrote on the last leaf of the record: "And
now I bid unto all, farewell. I soon go to rest in the paradise of my
God, until my spirit and body shall again reunite, and I am
brought forth triumphant through the air, to meet you
before the pleasing bar of the great Jehovah."
(Moroni 10:34).

With
faith as a grain of
mustard seed, we'll have a
germinating desire to engage
in a serious investigation of the
principles, doctrine, ordinances, and
covenants of The Book of Mormon, the
things that were among the "great and
eternal purposes (that) were prepared
from the foundation of the world."
(Alma 42:26). Our baptism itself
testifies that we were willing
then, and are eager now, to
ratify and participate in
God's great Plan of
Happiness.

Alma taught: "For behold, it is as
easy to give heed to the word of Christ,
which will point to you a straight course to
eternal bliss, as it was for our fathers to give
heed to this compass, which would point unto
them a straight course to the promised land."
(Alma 37: 44). As it was for Alma and his
people, so it is for us. The Book of Mormon
has become our 'rudder,' and the Savior
is our Navigator. If we follow it, and
Him, and allow them to guide us
to the waters of baptism, we'll
find that there is no wind
that can blow except
it fills our sails.

The bedrock that is
beneath our foundation in
the Kingdom of God supports
the footings of saving faith, as did
the wall that was built by an Irishman
around his farm. When asked why he had
erected it five feet high and eight feet thick, he
explained that if the wind ever blew so hard that
it would topple over, his wall of protection would
still be five feet thick. The Book of Mormon does
the same thing. It shelters us with the shield of
faith, enabling us to withstand any wind
that blows, no matter how ferocious or
terrifying it might seem to be.

We retain an abiding faith in the
Book of Mormon's glorious promise that,
because of our baptismal covenant, one day in
the not-too-distant future, the atmosphere that we
breathe will be pungent with a heavenly ether that is
punctuated by the melodious strains of an animated
conversation that is constructed in our native tongue.
Every detail will be exactly as we had imagined it to
be, including the heat radiating from a reassuring
celestial fire that has been kindled beforehand by
the Father of our spirits, in the anticipation
of our homecoming. (See Hosea 1:10,
Romans 8:16, Ephesians 4:6,
Hebrews 12:9, & 1 Nephi
17:36).

We are baptized so that the Spirit of the Lord God Omnipotent might work "a mighty change in us, or in our hearts, that we have no more disposition to do evil, but to do good continually." (Mosiah 5:2).

As they were baptized, angels attended the faithful Nephites. "For I will go before your face," promised the Savior. "I will be on your right hand, and on your left, and my Spirit shall be in your hearts, and mine angels round about you, to bear you up." (D&C 84:88). With such a promise, they determined to never turn their backs on such an outpouring of spiritual fortification, return to their wicked ways, fly solo, or try to make it on their own.

Those timid souls who remain cautiously hesitant and tentatively faithful don't consciously intend to ignore the spiritual promptings that urge them to boldly reach out and embrace The Book of Mormon. Faith to believe never takes root, or if it has, it just quietly fades away like a slow leak in a bike tire, rather than as a blowout.

There's nothing that's quite as powerful as our sins to motivate us to haul our broken and battered bodies to the gym that goes by the name of The Church of Jesus Christ of Latter-day Saints. For it is there, under the direction and guidance of priesthood fitness trainers, that we're encouraged to participate in the robust spiritual workouts that introduce us to their prominent regimens. These include an easy familiarity with the mission of the Prophet Joseph Smith, a testimony of The Book of Mormon, and most importantly of all, a relationship with our Lord and Savior Jesus Christ.

The Great Plan of the Eternal God (Alma 34:9), dictates that there will come for every one of us a great and dreadful day when we will be asked to stand and give our sworn deposition before God, angels, and witnesses. (See Alma 5:22). Upon the issue of faith, depending upon our answer, we will be counted among the sheep or the goats, and find ourselves on His right hand, or on His left hand.

The doctrine that can be found on nearly every page in The Book of Mormon constitutes "the words of eternal life" (John 6:63) and when followed, it has the power to emancipate us from the self-limiting conditions that had heretofore blinded us to a larger view of life. It will free us to pay close attention to celestial guideposts and principles. It invites us to experience more intense and reflective self-awareness, deeper and more abiding humility, reinvigorated confidence, and incomprehensibly more profound and enduring faith in our Savior Jesus Christ. Doctrine has the power to make our lives sublime as they turn on the hands of time.

The Book of Mormon will charge us with the power to follow the Savior "with full purpose of heart, acting no hypocrisy and no deception before God." (2 Nephi 31:13). When we do so, our long night of darkness will be followed by a renaissance, a spiritual rebirth paving the way for enlightenment. Our world will blossom with new ideas and with unbridled optimism, and we'll realize that it is we of whom Isaiah spoke: Although we once groped about in darkness, we have now seen a great light. We once dwelt in the valley of the shadow of death, but now, the Holy Ghost traces a flaming trajectory for us to follow as it streaks across an endless horizon. (See Isaiah 9:2).

In The Book of Mormon, the anchors of our faith rest upon a foundation of rock, rather than of sand. Our testimonies are composed of three essential elements. First is our deliberate recognition of gospel principles. Secondly, is our comprehensive understanding of the word of God concerning the principles. And finally, is our direct experience with said principles, which we call the fruits of faith.

If we no
longer believe in
The Book of Mormon,
we must concede that our
skepticism is attributable to
a lack of faith that initiated the
flat spin from which we could not
recover. Blame for the demolition of
our discipleship, not to mention the
cascade of catastrophic consequences
that follow, must come home to roost
at our own doorstep. When we try to
shift that culpability to others, we
are only deluding ourselves.

The Book
of Mormon will
help us to appreciate
that we are here, at this
place, and in this time, by
divine design. What we think
are only coincidences, if they are
instead viewed thru the clarifying
lens of eternity, are faith promoting
examples of the Lord patiently working
behind the scenes in our behalf. Nothing
in our lives happens by chance. While we
are not billiard balls, it is equally true
that most, if not all, of the things that
are of significance to us will happen
according to the perfect Plan of
our Heavenly Father.

It is
within the matrix
of the principles of The
Book of Mormon that we
will encounter a description of
the only truly effective shields of
protection against a corrosive spatter
of perspiration that is cast about by the
Devil, who pervasively and persistently
works overtime in a concentrated effort
to damage our doctrinal defenses, dull
our spiritual sensitivities, diminish
our charitable capacity, deplete
our bountiful reservoirs of
sympathy, and destroy
our devotions. (See
3 Nephi 4:30).

In The Book of Mormon, every
time that the Nephites fortified themselves
with righteousness, they were insulated from
the influences of the world that would have otherwise
left them vulnerable to the enticements of him who is the
adversary of all that is good. The terrible effect of sin on those
who had previously been taught the principles of the gospel was
that the guidance of the Spirit was withdrawn, leaving them to
to grope in darkness alone. Guilt caused them to shrink from
church fellowship, and in the absence of the Spirit, sinners
had little claim on blessings, prosperity, or preservation.
Tragically, those individuals, feeling uncomfortable
in proximity to spiritual experiences, withdrew to
lifestyles devoid of such associations. Thus
began a downward spiral that gained
momentum as sinful practices,
more easily committed,
became habitual.

"Blessed is the man (whose) delight is in the law of the Lord" as it is found, for example, in The Book of Mormon. For "he shall be like a tree planted by the rivers of water, that bringeth forth his fruit in his season; his leaf also shall not wither; and whatsoever he doeth shall prosper. The ungodly are not so, but are like the chaff which the wind driveth away. Therefore, the ungodly shall not stand in the judgment, nor sinners in the congregation of the righteous. For the Lord knoweth the way of the righteous: but the way of the ungodly shall perish."
(Psalms 1:1-6).

Heavenly Father's Great and Eternal Plan of Deliverance from Death (see 2 Nephi 11:5), has provisions that have been etched into its blueprints, stipulating that guidance from heaven will come to us in the form of subtle impressions and spiritual promptings that are more common that one might suspect. Powerful intuitive communicators influence us to push forward in the direction of our dreams, toward the faith to believe, that blesses us with a greater appreciation of the concern of our Savior for each of us, which brings us back to an equally significant name for His divine design, which is the Great Plan of Happiness.
(See Alma 42:8).

We need
to venture forth
out from the shadows,
and rely upon the guidance
that we've received from the Light
of Christ and from the ministering
of angels, if we want to experience the
special familiarity that the faithful enjoy
with the Lord of all the earth, and with "the
Great Plan of The Eternal God" of which,
and of Whom. the Spirit regularly
testifies. (Alma 39:4).

When
it's our time
to come face to
face with eternity
(see Moroni 10:34), the
principles of the Plan will
catalyze the transformation
of our mortal clay to something
that is "a better and an enduring
substance." (Hebrews 10:34). Thus,
for as long as we remain confined to
our bodies, it will be possible for us
to only indirectly recognize and
appreciate the eternal scope of
God's divine design.

As we study,
and we learn precept
by precept, here a little
and there a little the details
relating to the Great Plan that
God has devised for us, we realize
that we can become the architects of
our own destiny. But it also dawns on
us just how much we have borrowed from
our Lord Jesus Christ, as well as from the
towering examples of the prophets of The
Book of Mormon who have always been
our mystical mentors, as well as our
sensible chaperones, our spiritual
guides, our surrogate saviors,
our compassionate critics,
and our spiritual
guides.

If, as
we study The
Book of Mormon,
we have unknowingly
taken poetic license with
the foundation principles of
the book, or if we have needlessly
added ecclesiastical embroidery to
gospel truths, we risk diminishing
the intensity of our faith to believe,
and we must speedily repent, and
modify our approach to worship
and to gospel scholarship.

Armed
with our faith in
The Book of Mormon,
our innermost longings
to apprehend visions of the
eternal worlds are epitomized
by our triumphant awareness of
dreams fulfilled. In the expression
of our testimonies, our emotions will
be painted by words that describe our
progression toward distant mileposts
that mark the way we must all go as
we trudge along through the vast
wastelands of Idumea, past the
great and spacious buildings
of Babylon, on our way to
keep our promised date
with destiny.

The Book of Mormon has the
mystical power to surprise us in
myriad and delightful ways. It
cultivates a culture of reflection,
keeps the Savior in our thoughts,
nurtures an eternal perspective,
and initiates positive change,
while obedience to principles
helps us to harmonize our
our actions with the
order of heaven.

Those who have
become enslaved by
their selfish indulgences
to the point that they "regard
not the work of the Lord, neither
consider the operation of his hands,"
must ultimately drink of the wine of the
wrath of the indignation of God. (2 Nephi
15:12). Without knowledge of heaven, they are
as those who are "famished, and their multitude
dried up with thirst. Therefore, hell hath enlarged
herself, and opened her mouth without measure;
and their glory, and their multitude, and their
pomp, and he that rejoiceth, shall descend
into it (even as) God that is holy (is)
sanctified in righteousness."
(2 Nephi 15:13-16).

We learn from
The Book of Mormon
that following the ministry
of the Savior among the Nephites,
their love for Him, and for each other,
was so great that they were the happiest
people of all those who had ever been
created by the hand of God.
(See 4 Nephi 1:15-16).

The Book of Mormon gives us the tools to watch ourselves judiciously, that we might be the meticulous guardians of our thoughts, the scrupulous custodians of our words, and the prudent caretakers of our actions. We fastidiously observe the laws of God, that we might benefit from the stability of a pathway that basks in a steady illumination of truth that has been generously augmented by the dynamo of faith.

It can be all too easy to talk about our faith in The Book of Mormon timidly or superficially by retreating into tasteless and colorless verbiage as the easy way out. We take care that we are not steering a course that would take us away from the Savior by any inconsiderate, thoughtless, or dismissive expressions that might betray a weakness in the armor of our testimony.

If we've never allowed the stories from The Book of Mormon to give us the strength to endure the hard lessons that life throws our way with frustrating frequency, we'll look elsewhere for gods of wood and stone to heal our temporal trauma and our spiritual schizophrenia. But at our core, we'll know that these quick fixes lack power to redeem us from the sorrow in our hearts that is so often the consequence of a freefall from faith.

If we are too busy to study The Book of Mormon, it is likely because we have become absorbed in puerile activities that concentrate on obtaining, accumulating, consolidating, and securing our material interests. The problem with that juvenile approach to life is that the eternal welfare of our souls continues to hang in the balance, no matter where our misguided priorities may lie.

The Book
of Mormon
orders our chaotic
world, bequeathing
our lives with clarity
rather than confusion.
It simply teaches us how
to achieve fluency in the
intuitive language of
the Spirit.

Those who have
been enslaved by selfish
indulgences "drink out of the
cup of the wrath of God." (Mosiah
3:26). They "regard not the work of
the Lord, neither (do they) consider the
operation of his hands." (2 Nephi 15:12).
Without the knowledge of His ways, they
are held captive, are "famished, and their
multitude dried up with thirst. Therefore,
hell hath enlarged herself, and opened
her mouth without measure; and their
glory, and their multitude, and their
pomp, and he that rejoiceth, shall
descend into it (even as) God
that is holy (is) sanctified
in (His) righteousness."
(2 Nephi 15:13-16).

The Book of Mormon has the ability to bless our lives with self-shaping, self-supporting, self-sustaining and self-renewing characteristics. At its center, its doctrine becomes a perfectly liberating law that allows us to reach our potential in an atmosphere of mutually supportive inter-dependency with the Savior. His work and glory become our quest for the holy grail of immortality and eternal life in the Celestial Kingdom.

Those who are of weak character think that they might somehow find ways to circumvent the performance requirements of The Book of Mormon, but this is because they have never enjoyed the experiences of those who claim the strait and narrow way as their home turf. They mistake corrupt behavior for happiness, captivity for obedience, pleasure for the joy of the Lord, and nature for nobility. They see only a single dimension of the contraries that exist in the gospel of Jesus Christ, that can help us to be strong.

We talk about being "Best Friends Forever," but Heavenly Father would rather have us "Be Forever Faithful" through the bonds of obedience to the doctrines, principles, ordinances, and covenants that He wants us to discover for ourselves as we read, study, and pray about The Book of Mormon.

Within the embrace of group study of the magnificent themes running thru The Book of Mormon, conformity can provide each member with significant sustainable support. Without the consistency that is one of the great blessings of fellowship, our lives might hurl downward in a flat spin. Such is the condition of those who've been confronted by a sense of futility accompanying their solitary failure to concentrate on the innate upward thrust provided by the gospel to those who are seeking the truth.

Although we remain exasperatingly powerless to save our daylight time, we may still attempt to maximize it by strangling ourselves with the things that we can purchase, whose opacity obstructs our capacity to see what's really there. In fact, we aren't on daylight savings time at all, but rather on Book of Mormon time. We observe the Lord's agenda, for we're on His errand no matter how long it might take, or how preoccupied by the distractions and trivial concerns of the world we may have become. He wants us to spend our time wisely, and turn our attention to The Book of Mormon!

In The Book of Mormon, we're taught that our road to repentance will follow a natural progression, but the real power that stems from the Atonement and saves us from our sins hinges upon a deeper and more abiding faith. It is, Paul wrote, "the substance of things hoped for, (and) the evidence of things not seen." (Hebrews 11:1).

The Holy Ghost is able
to see through the clarifying
and purifying lens of eternity,
and from a unique vantage point.
He will bless our lives as He nurtures
our testimony of The Book of Mormon.
The veil that has been drawn before our
eyes prevents us for only a moment
from experiencing eternity from
the unobstructed viewpoint of
the thousand years of
Nephite history.

In The Book
of Mormon we are
taught that were it not
for the Atonement of Jesus
Christ, we would be devoid of
the blessings we receive because
of our obedience to covenants, and
we would remain miserable, living
in a state of separation, not only
from the presence of our Father
in Heaven, but also from His
only begotten Son, as well
as from the Holy
Ghost.

The Book of Mormon
motivates us to examine
what it means to be anxiously
engaged. It inspires us to plumb
the depths of our commitment to the
Savior. It sensitizes us to the nobility
of His work, expands upon our visions of
immortality, personalizes His Atonement,
and encourages us to remain consciously
aware of God's promise of immortality
and eternal life, and of our close
proximity to heaven.

It is
in The Book
of Mormon where
we learn that Jesus
Christ is the Father of
our spiritual regeneration
and that, like the parent we
all want to be, He'll be there to
heal our infirmities and bind
up our wounds, every time we
stumble and whenever we fall
because of the weight we have
been attempting to carry by
ourselves. Even though we
may forget about Him,
and try to go it alone,
He will never forget
about us.

The more righteous
individuals among the Nephites
bound themselves to the heavens by
their obedience, initializing a pulsing
stream of inspiration whose flow knew
neither temporal boundaries nor spatial
limitations. When they were bad, they
were very bad, but when they were
good, they were at one with the
mind and will of God. And
that is why His arm is
stretched out
still.

Since there must
needs be opposition, even as
there's faith, so must there also be
its worldly counterpart. In our own
day, the awful grip of fear paralyzes
many of God's children. Today, more
than ever, we need a hope in Christ. We
need the assurance of peace, that our
lives are moving in the direction
of our dreams. In The Book of
Mormon, we are taught how
to lasso the stars, to turn
our dreams into
reality,.

The
Book of
Mormon shows
how to see with the
eye of faith, as thru
a spiritual prism. It's
principles will touch us,
so that we may learn to see
beyond the limited horizon
of our sight, all the way into
the eternities. By the power of
the Holy Ghost, our eyes will
be opened, that we may begin
to understand the reach of
the Savior's influence
over our lives.

We
are blessed
to internalize
the doctrine between
the covers of The Book
of Mormon, but only after
our faith has been religiously
recalibrated thru repentance. It
allows us to become reinvigorated
by the refreshing breeze of celestial
air. Its teachings paint a portrait of
free-will where we may take risks. If,
in our efforts, we fail to measure up
to our obligations, Jesus Christ will
always step in to intervene in our
behalf by using the bargaining
chip of His Atonement in order
to placate the unrelenting
demands of Justice.

It is our faith that binds together the doctrinal building blocks that are found within The Book of Mormon's pages. Without it, the fabric of our lives unravels in a process leading to disintegration. When the anchor of the knowledge of the Plan of God is missing, our experiences can be like a train wreck in slow motion that is frustratingly repeated over and over in an endless cycle.

In the Twenty-first Century, a daunting challenge we face when we are introduced to The Book of Mormon is to somehow temper our insatiable desire for pleasure, for immediate gratification, and for repetitive waves of greater and greater stimulation. We are frustrated by the limitations of our RAM, the horsepower of our autos, the features of our cell phones, and the speed of our micro-processors. We have only a dim recollection of typewriters and white-out, operator assistance, two-lane country roads, and sipping lemonade on a lazy summer afternoon while seated in a rocker on the front porch. As society demands escalating criteria to maintain its false standard of comfort and entertainment, we are blinded to the sobering comparison to a heroin addict's progressive tolerance and destructive reliance on false gods of wood and stone, and drugs. Materialism is a cholesterol that clogs our spiritual arteries. The angioplasty of The Book of Mormon liberates us to regain our perspective, and strengthens our reverence for God's work.

Mormon taught us that obstacles are frightful demons that threaten us when we take our minds off the Atonement. They loom large with a gratuitous significance. It is faith that endows us with the vision to see beyond these potential stumbling blocks. If we turn them into stepping stones to pave the way to our higher achievement, it will be because we've been empowered by the capacity of our hope in Jesus Christ, that is an unrestrained and creative engine that drives positive change. His truth will make us free. (See John 8:32).

Sooner or later, each of us must undertake a journey that will lead to The Book of Mormon. As we move along the Yellow Brick Road thru the forest of faith toward the Emerald City of Oz, we use the brains we've been given to infuse our hearts with courage, all the while remembering that the woods would be very quiet if no birds sang but those that sang best.

Without
knowledge,
there can be no
faith; without faith,
there can be no light,
and without light there
cannot be a recognition of
religious truth; and without
spiritual enlightenment, when
just one of these three elements
of faith, light, and truth is lost,
then all must be forsaken. Our
fortunes rest upon the basis of
how completely we internalize
this fundamental teaching
of the prophets from The
Book of Mormon.

The Book
of Mormon is as
our celestial compass,
calibrated by God's finger.
It is oriented toward the truth,
and it is always available to guide
the faithful to a safe haven. It is also
there for those who have lost their way,
to bring them into the fold of the Good
Shepherd, and to show others how they
might return to the sanctuary and
security of the community of
Christ from which they
may have strayed.

Those who decline to nurture and then maintain a deep and abiding faith in the doctrinal truth of The Book of Mormon lack spiritual horsepower. Their dearth of traction is awkwardly apparent while the inability to generate spontaneity is palpable, and their lack of energy to engage enthusiasm is noticeable. Their incapacity to spark vitality is apparent, and their failure to unabashedly acknowledge the dynamic relationship that can exist between God and themselves is indisputable.

Just as drug addicts keep on coming back for one more fix, the wicked continue to demand signs from the ministers of the Lord as proof of their authority. (See Jacob Chapter 7 & Alma Chapter 30). Those with adulterous hearts seek signs for the satisfaction of desires that require an increasing intensity of validation for the same level of gratification. But, at times, signs are given for no reason other than to vindicate prophetic warning. Because consequences naturally follow actions, signs may be given to establish our accountability. But in every case, the wicked are left holding the bag, with responsibility for their indefensible behavior, without regard to their acceptance or rejection of the signs that may be in question.

Sooner or later, each of us, as a child of God, must discover for ourselves that a line has been drawn in the sand. If we then act upon the promptings of the Holy Ghost to seize the power of The Book of Mormon, we will generate the positive energy that will move us inexorably forward in the direction of our dreams. Those with the faith to rely upon the merits of Christ, of Whom the book so boldly testifies, will never cross over that line, for they wish to be saved in the kingdom of God.

We will receive no witness until after the trial of our faith. Having said that, those with little or no faith will characteristically throw up defensive dross that is designed to deflect, disrespect, disregard, discourage, or even disparage the power of The Book of Mormon. They may be enthusiastic, but they are still ignorant.

How
we choose to go
about generating
the faith to believe in
The Book of Mormon will
either deify or destroy us.
Our response to the Savior's
entreaties to come unto Him
will define our destiny and
delineate our dreams, and
will determine how, where
and with whom we will
spend all eternity. We
can almost hear the
voice of the Lord
as He exclaims:
'Carpe diem!'

There will come for each
of us a great and dreadful day,
when we will be asked to stand and
face God, angels, and witnesses, to give
our sworn deposition. On the issue of faith
in The Book of Mormon, Another Testament
of Christ, depending on our statement, we'll
be counted among the sheep or the goats, and
find ourselves on His right hand, or on His
left hand. We should begin thinking about
how we will respond to the gentle inquiry:
"What think ye of Christ? Whose Son
is He? and "What think ye of The
Book of Mormon?"

In The Book of Mormon, and more particularly in the account of Christ's New World ministry in Third Nephi, we're reminded of the suffering of our Savior when He took upon Himself the heavy burden of our sins, and so it stimulates our own soul-sweat. It works upon our sense of duty, on our conscience, and on our scruples, and it persistently persuades us to act on our faith, so that not our will, but that of God, might be done.

The Nephites' wicked Lamanite brethren, who wouldn't repent, had a taste for doctrinal fast-food that had just been heated up for ten seconds in a sensory microwave. It was only outwardly appealing and was full of empty calories. When the Lamanites measured the missionaries and their message of salvation, they tended to see darkly, through a filter of worldly pollution that had been desperately, but superficially, whitewashed to cover up the underlying canker in their character.

One of the greatest blessings that continues to flow from our unequivocal acceptance of The Book of Mormon, is our concurrent receipt of a constant stream of inspiration that cascades down from the heavens. This ensures that we will walk along illuminated pathways guided by the only institution that has the right to legitimately claim that it receives revelation, and that has been given God's approbation, even The Church of Jesus Christ of Latter-day Saints.

Since Mormon knew that Babylon's image consultants would confuse the weightier matters of the law in the tumultuous Last Days, he cautioned us to "take heed, that (we) not judge that which is evil to be of God, or that which is good and of God to be of the devil." (Moroni 7:14). In the vast arena of the world, there are no shades of gray for those who have not only received the Light of Christ, but also the greater illumination of the Holy Ghost. To them it is given "to judge, that (they) may know good from evil; and the way to judge is as plain, that ye may know with a perfect knowledge, as the daylight is from the dark night." (Moroni 7:15).

The Book of Mormon furnishes us with more than enough doctrinal calories to satisfy all the dietary entrance requirements for admittance into God's kingdom. We couldn't be blessed with a greater gift to help us to control our spiritual appestat than the Holy Ghost, Who stands ready to serve as our celestial nutritional consultant.

Every one of us has been exposed to a constant stream of insight and intuition, as well as of inspiration and revelation that flows in cascading creativity from its Source. Heavenly supervision blesses all of us to walk along illuminated pathways and to execute our faculties of mind and spirit, to better utilize The Book of Mormon to meet the challenges of the day.

The familiar phrase 'isles of the sea' that is found in the scriptures is an antiquated Semitic expression describing the practice of sailing to far-away places. The continents of Africa and Asia, by contrast, were characterized as 'the earth,' because they were accessible by land. Idioms are expressions that are peculiar to a given culture, and we would expect Semitic instances throughout The Book of Mormon. The facility with which they have been sprinkled into its narrative suggests that they were devices that were frequently employed by legitimate Israelite authors. It begs credulity to suggest that Joseph Smith was so adept that, on his own initiative, he would have known how to utilize Semitic colloquialisms throughout the record, not to mention how to apply each one in an undeniably perfect literary and cultural context.

Obedience to principles that are elucidated in The Book of Mormon will release us from both intellectual and spiritual captivity, allowing us to see things as they really are, and to enjoy a lucidity that stems more from our hearts, than from our heads.

The Book of Mormon will prepare us for an exciting journey along a pathway that leads to the Kingdom of God. Those of us who embrace its teachings await the further light and knowledge that He has promised to send us through His prophets.

As if they were our spiritual swaddling clothes, the threads of faith that have been woven into our coats of many colors reverberate with intrinsic light from The Book of Mormon. It radiates in a pulsing stream whose trail is traceable all the way to a witness of the Spirit.

As we reflect upon the
implications of our lineage
and birthright that we learn
about in The Book of Mormon,
we might want to consider our
own covenant consciousness,
and never forget that we, too,
are members of the House of
Israel, either literally or by
adoption, and that we too
may claim the covenant
blessings promised by
God so long ago, not
only to Abraham,
but also, to all
of his seed.

Angels, who have
been commissioned to the work,
are the servants of Jesus Christ. The
office of their ministry is to call us "unto
repentance, and to fulfil and to do the work of
the covenants of the Father, which he hath made
unto the children of men, to prepare the way by
declaring the word of Christ unto the chosen
vessels of the Lord, that they may
bear testimony of him."
(Moroni 7:31).

One of the
terrible consequences
of the fascination of Babylon
with telestial titillation, and with
its fixation on the vain and trifling
images of the world, is its insensitivity
to spiritual impressions and whisperings
that it might have received had it been even
remotely interested in learning more about
the eternity-altering ramifications having
to do with internalizing the doctrine and
principles that are clearly illustrated
by the prophets of God who bore their
testimonies in nearly every
chapter of The Book
of Mormon.

For
various and
sundry reasons,
those of us who have
been given the supernal
gift of The Book of Mormon
may leave it undisturbed in its
original packaging. Some of us
never learned that, within its pages,
the Savior's guidance will help us as we
make important choices. We learn how to
keep our covenants with God by engaging
its principles and doctrine, that are all a
part of His Great Plan of Salvation.

In The Book of Mormon, we are taught that from the foundation of the world, the Atonement of Jesus Christ initiated the preparation of a petition that will be submitted to the court of Justice, seeking a summary dismissal of all of the charges that have been lodged against us. Our trial proceedings have already been docketed to follow the conclusion of our mortal experience. To avoid a reversal of our fortunes, we must pay our Advocate the retainer of a broken heart and a contrite spirit, for He is even now preparing to plead our case at the commencement of that heavenly tribunal.

Every one of the willing participants in life's Three Act Play is now and forever independent in that stage of development to which their decisions have led them. Poised at the edge of forever, they need little incentive other than the encouragement of Moroni (see Moroni 10:32), to cast themselves off in the direction of the unknown possibilities of existence, where they will seek out new life and new civilizations, and boldly go to a place where no one but the faithful have gone before.

It is God's work and glory for all His children, sooner or later, to make their way to Christ, and a good way to do that is to start right now by following the guidance provided in The Book of Mormon. If they do that, it will be as it was during the reign of King Josiah, who "went up into the house of the Lord, and all the men of Judah and all the inhabitants of Jerusalem with him, and the priests, and the prophets, and all the people, both small and great. And (they) made a covenant before the Lord, to walk after the Lord, and to keep his commandments and his testimonies and his statutes with all their heart and all their soul, (and) to perform the words of the covenant. And all the people stood to the covenant." (2 Kings 23:2-3).

As we study the scriptures and we consider the elements of all of the references to God's Creation that are found in The Book of Mormon, for example, in 1 Nephi 17:36, 2 Nephi 2:14 & 29:7, Jacob 2:21 & 4:9, Mosiah 2:21, 3:8, 4:9 & 7:27, & Alma 18:28-32, it seems that our faith should remain fixed on the revelations the Lord has given us that relate to our world, and not on mysteries that have not been revealed to us, may never be revealed, or that just may not be pertinent to our current circumstances.

If
we'll read The
Book of Mormon to
gain a testimony of the
truth, we'll face the sun, that
we might feel the warmth of its
rays upon our cheeks. We'll listen
with greater sensitivity, hear the word
of the Lord without ambiguity, and see
with a lucidity that encourages us to turn
a deaf ear to those who are at different mile
posts on their own journeys, who curse the
darkness at noonday, lament that the
heavens are silent, and teach that
prophecy has ceased to exist.

While they drew, a kindergarten teacher
walked up and down the rows of students in her
class, observing her pupils' work. She paused at the
desk of a little girl and asked what she was drawing.
She replied: "I'm drawing a picture of God." The teacher
paused, and then tentatively said: "But no one knows
what He looks like." Without missing a beat, or even
looking up from her paper, the girl said: "They
will in a minute." Though she was tender in
years, this child had faith (and her
parents had probably read
The Book of Mormon
to her).

If we want to capture the blessings that are manifest within the sacramental prayers that are spelled out with exactness in Moroni Chapters 4 & 5, to always have the Spirit to be with us, we'll need to experience how the Holy Ghost demonstrates personal revelation. "For God speaketh once, yea twice, yet man perceiveth it not. In a dream, in a vision of the night, when deep sleep falleth upon men, in slumberings upon the bed; then he openeth the ears of men, and sealeth their instruction." (Job 33:4-16).

If it is our desire to sustain our focus of faith while we investigate the claims made by The Book of Mormon, we won't get in the thick of thin things. We'll cultivate an equilibrium centered away from the madding crowd and at a safe distance that's far from the ego-filled minds of mediocre men. We'll do our best to insulate ourselves from the confusion and tumult of the world, in the hope that we might enjoy a firmness of fidelity to God that is unshakable.

All of those who have forsaken the world to faithfully embrace The Book of Mormon, adopt the gospel of Jesus Christ, and internalize the lifestyle of Latter-day Saints, have experienced spiritual heart transplants. Therefore, anti-rejection protocols must be rigorously observed after they have been given their new hearts, and have been born again.

When he spoke to members of the church who dwelt in Corinth, the apostle Paul painted a vivid portrait of our own second mile commitment of faith after we have gained a testimony of The Book of Mormon and the great latter-day work. He asserted that we "are manifestly declared to be the epistle of Christ ministered by us, written not with ink, but with the Spirit of the living God; (and not just) in tables of stone, but (also) in fleshy tables of the heart." (2 Corinthians 3:3).

As we study The
Book of Mormon, and our
minds and our hearts begin to
grasp the nature of God, we learn
more about how we fit in to His divine
design. We discover how faith drives the
law into our inward parts. We intuitively
sense this, and when the procedure has been
accomplished, in one of His tender mercies,
the articles of our faith will have become the
particles of our faith, and we will have
become new creatures in Christ, in a
process of generation, and not
just of maturation.

The tendency
toward turmoil can
be a tell-tale sign that
the Deceiver is lurking in
the shadows, lying in wait to
disrupt the poise of those who are
pressing forward in the direction of
the dreams lying at the very core of the
divine center of their faith. They'll need to
lift the latch and force the way, even as they
ponder and pray about the prodigious themes
running through The Book of Mormon..

Baptism initiates both the temporal and spiritual elements of God's Plan. Our baptismal covenant allows us to continually monitor our relationship with Him during our engagement with mortality. Our salvation hinges upon a correct understanding of the points of doctrine that focus on our salvation, and that are clearly illustrated in The Book of Mormon.

There are those who are in our midst who are nothing more than modern scribes and Pharisees. They have little or no faith, and omit the weightier matters of the law, including the metal plates from which The Book of Mormon was translated by the gift and power of God. They strain at a gnat, and swallow a camel, appearing to be pious, but inside they are "full of extortion and excess." (Matthew 23:25). At the other end of the spectrum, it's the righteous desire of the pure in heart to exercise the wisdom of faith to bring themselves closer to the Savior, leaving scant room for hypocrisy to creep into their behavior. Somehow, they have managed to forge a spiritual bond with the Infinite.

Book of Mormon prophet-
historians have provided us with the
practical skills that teach us how to express
ourselves through positive and independent
action, while the courage of faith introduces
us to the exhilarating feeling of freedom
from incarceration to sin that we can
only experience when we have been
obedient to a Higher Power, and
we have received forgiveness
for our sins through the
Atonement of Jesus
Christ.

The
Savior's ministry
among the Nephites after
His resurrection from the dead
may be one the greatest miracles
of all, but those who deny the Lord's
divinity can't be saved on His merits
alone, because they have not generated
faith with enough power to convey their
progression onward. Only a profound
adjustment in attitude that takes into
consideration every element of God's
Plan of Salvation could jump-start
their discipleship with the forward
momentum to carry them along
a pathway via the Atonement
that leads directly to the
Kingdom of God.

"Behold, the field was ripe," cried Ammon to his fellow missionaries Aaron, Omner, and Himni, "and blessed are ye, for ye did thrust in the sickle, and did reap with your might, yea, all the day long did ye labor (for fourteen long years!) and behold the number of your sheaves!" (Alma 26:5). His party had come up out of the Land of Zarahemla into the highlands of Nephi to bring a message of love to the Lamanites. In the absence of their invitation to their brethren to embrace the first principles and ordinances of the gospel, they "would still have been racked with hatred (against their Nephite kinsmen and) would also have (remained in the dark as) strangers to God." (Alma 26:9, see Ephesians 2:19).

While The Book of Mormon has the capability to stimulate the development of personality traits that are harmonious, or in balance, with the symmetry of heaven, sinful behavior is harmful because it interferes with our capacity to cultivate the equilibrium that is a defining characteristic of those who strive to inherit eternal life. In our deeds, there must be neither variableness, nor can God tolerate even the hint of a "shadow of turning." (James 1:17).

Zenos foresaw that Israel, characterized as the natural branches from an olive tree which had grown wild, was to be grafted in to the natural tree in a spiritual rebirth. Both the roots and branches would be equal in strength as they were nourished due to the word of the Lord, receiving line line upon line and precept upon precept. Covenant Israel, or the Gentiles, would grow up beside Blood Israel with a testimony of the Lord. In the millennial day, it will no longer be as before, when the branches had grown faster than the roots could bear.

God never promised the Nephites "skies always blue or flower-strewn pathways all their lives through. Nor has He promised sun without rain, joy without sorrow, or peace without pain. But He did promise them strength for the day, rest from their labors, and light for the way, grace for their trials, help from above, unfailing sympathy, and undying love." (Anonymous).

We are encouraged in The Book of Mormon to be perfect in our repentance, that God might give us the spirit of wisdom and of revelation to enlighten our understanding, so that we might embrace a hope of the high calling of Jesus Christ. Chariots of fire will then carry us heavenward, where we will commune with angelic beings, the general assembly, and the church of the Firstborn. (See 3 Nephi 28:13 & 2 Kings 2:11).

Because of Christ's Atonement we may remember our transgression of the law of God only in the positive sense that our testimony is increased. With the principle of opposition in all things, our Father in Heaven uses both sin and repentance to strengthen us to be more stalwart soldiers in the army of Christ. (Nephi 2:11, see Alma Chapter 42). Thus, even our disobedience will ultimately accrue to our benefit as well as to God's advantage.

After we
have fervently prayed
about the grand themes
that are found within in The
Book of Mormon, our faith will
convict us of our sins. Then, as we
approach the font, we'll bow our heads
in reverence. The words of the baptismal
prayer will orient our thoughts on the stars
to focus them on eternity, no matter where we
may have been bobbing about on the vast ocean
of life. Initially, getting a fix on the symbolism
that will come alive with intentional imagery and
magical metaphor might seem daunting to us. But
soon, the timeless messages that are conveyed by the
Spirit and have come down from the wide expanse
of heaven will descend upon us as the "dews of
Carmel" (D&C 128:19), transcending time,
and peacefully resting upon our minds.
God's tender mercies will loom larger
than life itself. (See 1 Nephi
1:20).

Once we have read The
Book of Mormon, have prayed
about it, and have received our own
witness of its divine authenticity, we
will have little inclination to look back
as we flee the lifestyle of Sodom and the
temptations of Gomorrah. (See Genesis
Chapters 18 & 19). We'll leave the ranks
of all those who have nestled themselves
into their vacation retreats in Idumea
amid pillars of salt, even though
their home addresses may still
be somewhere in Zion.

Those who surrender their dreams and deny the marvelous origin of The Book of Mormon sell their birthright to the lowest bidders for a mess of pottage. Once they have made the exchange, they may far too easily be dragged down to a hell on earth, where, with terror, they realize that it is with the spurious currency of the Devil, that great deceiver, that they've been paid, and that the only home they can now afford is the prison cell into which they have unceremoniously been cast.

Our acceptance of The Book of Mormon as scripture commits us to the arduous process of choosing the harder right, that is accompanied by a spiritual rebirth. Its alternative would leave us to follow a wobbly course that leads to the easier wrong. But that is a devilish detour that is characterized by the desire to subvert the Plan of God by forcing the capitulation by Mercy to a miscarriage of Justice, wherein we would somehow be saved in our sins.

When we allow
it to work its magic,
The Book of Mormon will
charge the air in the theater
of life as fire in the sky, with
electrical current representing the
inevitable merger of the universal
encouragement of the Light of
Christ with the pointed and
providential guidance of
the Holy Ghost, that is
God's gift of faith
to believe.

Any
attempts to
comprehend the
doctrine of The Book
of Mormon helps us to
understand ourselves. It
is when we have discovered
the answers to where we came
from and why we are here that
we'll be prepared to embark upon
the incredible journey into our
future, to see with the eye of
faith just where it is that
we are going.

With faith
to embrace the
harder right, while
distaining the easier
wrong, we will avoid the
world's amusement parks,
while appreciatively utilizing
the first aid stations described in
The Book of Mormon that have been
providentially provided for the use of
Zion's inhabitants. We will adapt its
teachings to be as a celestial barometer
that has been calibrated to a scale that
measures the capacity of our
hearts.

The Book
of Mormon is like
a fire in our bones, and it
causes our blood to run hot. It
is reminiscent of the microwave
background radiation which is an
ever-present reminder of the creation
of our universe billions of years ago,
as well as of the fiery cauldrons of
experience that were catalyzed in
a garden setting eastward in
Eden, that was not so
very long ago.

In
The Book
of Mormon
(3 Nephi 9:15), we
learn that it was Jesus
Christ, under the direction
of our Father in Heaven, Who
created the earth upon which we
stand as a learning laboratory and
as a telestial testing center. It would
be a citadel of higher education, and a
home where we would be blessed to have
all of the tools that could conceivably
be necessary to validate God's faith
in us; to see if we could muster an
equivalent faith in His Plan for
us, and in the infinite and
eternal Atonement
of His Son.

When we
have stockpiled
sufficient assets in
our spiritual savings
accounts, when they are
nearing depletion, or even
if our accounts are overdrawn,
the financial institution whose
reserves are securely deposited in
The Book of Mormon will still be
there to distribute pennies from
heaven, or the currency of
faith in its myriad
forms.

The sinews of our loins will resonate with recognition when we encounter the doctrine of The Book of Mormon. In this way, each of us has been blessed with the innate capacity to hearken to the voice of the Spirit, even the Holy Ghost, that one day we might return to the warm embrace of our Father, Who waits for us in heaven.

Astute observers have posited the supposition that society has paid a heavy price because it lacks a faithful focus on the gift of The Book of Mormon together with the restoration of the gospel. They are proposing that its spiritual equilibrium has become disoriented because its moral compass is spinning wildly out of control. That pessimistic assessment explains why its values appear to be undergoing repetitive readjustment in an unconscious, misguided, and vain attempt to regain a state of balance between the stratospheric stability of heaven and the inexorable tendency to entropy of earth. Its flat spin that is headed to destruction will only be corrected through the steadying application of the correct principles of spiritual aeronautical engineering that are obedient to doctrine overwhelming the 2nd law of thermodynamics.

Those who are lazy in their gospel discipleship and will not make the study of The Book of Mormon their daily habit, might well ask: "What do I want out of life?" while those of faith inquire: "What would Father have me do?" At a basic level, idleness is the devil's workshop, and so our refusal to be up and doing in the wake of the restoration of the gospel is sin. It is wasting our precious opportunities for renewal in fruitless pursuits when we should have been engaged in other and more worthy activities for which we've been blessed with God-given capabilities.

By allowing ourselves to be habitually distracted by trifling concerns until they've become the center of our attention and even our obsession, we ignore our innate desire to exercise our faith to believe in the heaven-sent origins of The Book of Mormon, and thereby we commit a grievous sin of omission.

It is the
false gods of
secular humanism
and similar ideologies
that extoll the virtues of the
intellect and demand tangible
proof that destroy our faith in
Jesus Christ. As Alma taught
the Zoramites, they will divert
us from following a Plan whose
successful execution hinges
upon nourishing the seeds
of innocent faith in its
capacity to save us
from our sins.

A testimony
of the truthfulness of
the doctrine in The Book of
Mormon includes three essential
elements. Initially, we are introduced
to the principle, as we earnestly study the
scriptures that are related to it. Second, is
our correct understanding of the counsel
of the Lord concerning the principle,
that comes with illumination that
we receive from the Holy Ghost.
And lastly, is our experience
with the principle, which is
the fruits of faith. (See
Galatians 5:2).

The fabric of our faith in the divine origin of The Book of Mormon can be traced back to the spiritual swaddling clothes that have been integrated into our coats of many colors. It is a faith resonating with intrinsic light, betraying the fact that its vibrancy is due to more than just pigment and dye. It comes from the Holy Ghost.

Our study of The Book of Mormon leads to purposeful performance. It must involve a vital, personal commitment to practical belief. But at the end of the day, our good works lack the efficacy of salvation. Faith in the Savior of the world is what activates God's grace in our behalf, and it is that power alone that will save us, after all we can do of ourselves.

When we stand before the pleasing Bar of God, the evidence will be presented, and our previous conformity to or rejection of eternal law will determine our reward or punishment. However, our innate capacity to have generated faith in the divine origin of Book of Mormon doctrine, due to the influences of the Light of Christ and the Holy Ghost, will make our mortal experiences more than just a roll of the dice. At the Bar, we will finally understand that our lives hadn't been a zero-sum game, after all. In fact, the cards had been marked and the deck stacked in our favor. Life hadn't been a game of chance, but rather an exercise involving skill. It was meant to be an exciting adventure, overseen by God, for knowledge is power, which renders the Judgment a win-win for both Him and His obedient children . (See Jacob 6:13 & Moroni 10:34).

As disciples, we are never ashamed to "declare (God's) doing among the people." Without embarrassment, it's easy "to make mention that His name is exalted." (2 Nephi 22:4). We join with our fellow Saints who have chosen to "stand as witnesses of God at all times and in all things, and in all places ... even unto death." (Mosiah 18:9).

When we
learn the language
of The Book of Mormon
(and especially of 2 Nephi
Chapters 12-24) we'll be blessed
with comprehension of a celestial
vernacular that is soothing to our
ears and calming to our souls. The
voice of the Spirit will be rhythmical
and melodious. As we hear it quietly
whisper: "You're a stranger here," it
will be comforting, as we discover
that we "have wandered from
a more exalted sphere."
(Eliza R. Snow).

An investment
in the study of The
Book of Mormon provides
us with a handsome return,
and with currency sufficient
for our needs, but it also allows
us, if we so choose, to substitute its
legal tender for stacks of counterfeit
cash with which late payments may be
made, with interest and penalties tacked
on to our debt as a necessary consequence
of bad behavior. Under those circumstances,
it could even be that our lease on life would be
threatened with cancellation for nonpayment
of the charges and levies that accumulate
as we conduct our business in the circus
of commerce on credit, rather than on
the cash basis of the Atonement,
for Jesus has already paid
for our sins.

We can
enlarge the
foundations of
our spiritual center,
and also make room for
our faith, even if the part
we've been asked to play in
the drama of our lives seems
awkward. After we have signed
our contract and we join other cast
members in the production of God's
Plan, we are reinvigorated to vividly
roleplay, to animatedly preplay, and
to repetitively replay the lines we have
been asked to deliver in the theater of
life. Rehearsals that are directed by
the Spirit will give us courage to be
worthy understudies to the Star of
the show, Who has unequivocally
been revealed within The Book of
Mormon to be none other than
our Lord and our Savior,
Jesus Christ.

When we
don't repent, the
Holy Spirit, which
burns like a fire, will
be quenched (see Alma
34:33), and the sacrifice
of the Savior will lose its
power to save us from
our sins.

The
tenets of
The Book of
Mormon carry
us in positive and
meaningful ways to
green pastures where we
enjoy the warm embrace of
the Good Shepherd, and where
we're permitted to experience the
intimate touch of His garment,
even if we sometimes feel that
we are lost in the press of the
crowd as He passes by.

The Nephites'
failure to repent was
a form of rebellion against
the Plan of Redemption of our
Heavenly Father. As was the case
following Lucifer's insurgency,
there needed to be consequences,
even if they had the potential
to be eternally damaging
in their scope.

In a classic demonstration of His magnificent omniscience, Father in Heaven negotiated with Justice from a position of power, because He had beforehand conceived the Atonement, in order to make possible the metamorphosis of His imperfect children to beings of light, and that includes both the Nephites and Lamanites of this world.

Alma taught his brethren in Zarahemla that it is our purpose in life to grow in grace, that we might progress in stature until we reach the point that we have developed both the image and likeness of our Heavenly Father. (See Alma 5:14).

The
Book
of Mormon
has extended a
wonderful blessing
to the faithful: Perfect
repentance witnessed by
the Spirit of Justification,
that compels us to consider
the possibility that, by the
grace of God, we might
one day actually be
holy and without
spot, as is our
Lord and
Savior.

Whenever we
attempt to shirk
the demands that the
Spirit puts upon us when
we've been invited to try the
virtue of God's word (see Alma
31:5), we risk being swallowed
up by a leviathan that is no less
real than the one that confronted
Jonah. If that proves to be the case,
we must then reluctantly resign
ourselves to eventually be spit
out upon the rocky shoreline
of our doubts, fears, and
apprehensions.

The world seeks change by exerting external controls, and fails miserably. The Book of Mormon, however, takes an innovative approach and influences the inner vessel, succeeding wonderfully by recalibrating our internal compass so that we might remain oriented toward the principles of the gospel.

The raw and ugly soul scars that are the festering residue of unresolved sinful behavior are incompatible with the uncompromising standard of prophylaxis or spiritual hygiene that's been made possible by the Atonement, and that is required, of those whose desire it, is to one day inhabit the heavens, to live in the company of both God and angels. (See Alma 5:21).

Joseph Smith could have been referring to The Book of Mormon, when he declared: "This is good doctrine. It tastes good. I can taste the principles of eternal life, and so can you. They are given to me by the revelations of Jesus Christ; and I know that ... you believe them. I can taste the spirit of eternal life. I know it is good, and when I tell you of these things which were given me by inspiration of the Holy Spirit, you are bound to receive them as sweet, and rejoice" as well.

It immediately captures our attention when those who mock The Book of Mormon wrest the scriptures. Those who do so will sometimes suggest with a misinterpretation of the teachings of the prophets that we are saved by works, twisting holy writ from its true or proper signification, and perverting it from its correct application. Make no mistake, however. We are saved by the grace of God, and by that alone.

The
Book of Mormon
helps us to redefine
and redesign what had
heretofore been stumbling
blocks; they are repurposed
into the very stepping stones
that are needed to conquer our
fears, to bolster our confidence,
and to overcome the obstacles
that are strewn all about
along the path of our
progression.

The
principles
and doctrines of
The Book of Mormon
were the foundation of
our pre-mortal classroom
curriculum. The incentive
to initiate decisive action
rests with each one of us,
and it is the Spirit that
invites us to experience
religious recognition,
or the re-knowing of
things we have
beforehand
learned.

As we commence our
Book of Mormon study, our pre-
existing limiting beliefs can blind
and deafen us to the mentors who might
have otherwise helped us to build our faith.
They can foster insensitivity to the standards
to which we might have, in other circumstances,
been drawn. They can corrode the iron rods that
run straight and true that might have otherwise
led us to the waters of baptism, and they can
weaken our focus on the absolutes in which
the Holy Ghost asks us to place our
unconditional trust.

To accomplish
its purpose, The Book
of Mormon requires us to
take God's labor of love and
somehow ease onto a world stage
that is lit only by fire. As we read
and study, our yearning to reach the
most holy faith that has been envisioned
by Heavenly Father is amplified, so that
a comfortable connection with the Holy
Ghost might be created, as well as a
relationship with our Lord, of
Whom the book testifies.

The Book of Mormon has the capacity to order our chaotic world, and to bless our lives with clarity rather than confusion. It simply teaches us how to be fluent in the language of the Spirit.

Our Father in Heaven celebrates the possibility that we might one day be like Him, and offers us His grace (see Moroni 10:32), consisting of the gifts and power by which we may be brought to His perfection and stature, so that we may enjoy not only what He has, but also what He is.

In every epoch of the history of the world, the tender shoots of budding testimony have sprung up and have been carefully nurtured in accord with Alma's inspired formula (see Alma Chapter 30), without the ecclesiastical embroidery that too often needlessly complicates the simple sewing, and the sowing, of the messages of the gospel.

In an ancient parable that we can relate to our own day, Israel was likened unto an olive tree with many branches that had broken off, only to be "scattered upon all the face of the earth." (1 Nephi 10:12). Lehi learned from the Spirit that his family group would be one of those branches that would be led from its homeland at Jerusalem to its own land of promise, that it might personify the fruitful bough by the well that had been prophesied by Jacob. (See Genesis 49:22).

Zion and Babylon will always be diametrically opposed, and remain as polarized camps at opposite ends of the spiritual spectrum. They are now, and forever will be, completely at odds with each other. There is little common ground upon which a substantive dialogue could ever be introduced, because the solid foundation pillars of Zion are simply philosophically incompatible with the detritus scattered about by the forces of Babylon, that was a repercussion from the War in Heaven. The theology upon which a Zion society is based has been articulated by Book of Mormon prophets. It allows its inhabitants to raise their eyes to God for redemption, while the world's apologists and political pundits cannot see beyond the intellect of man for their salvation, and can do little more than shrug their shoulders in resignation when they hear the clarion call to amend their behavior and focus their faith.

Our faith in the wise counsel of Book of Mormon prophets can vitalize the moral fiber we need to face our demons.

Evidence of the exercise of
our faith is revealed in how we will
receive The Book of Mormon. We gain
spiritual maturity until our faith becomes
perfect knowledge. Initially, faith is to believe
what we do not see, and the reward of faith is
to see what we believe. The process by which
faith is developed is one of testing. The
Lord gives certain principles, and by
obedience to them, blessings
and power follow.

It is because of The Book
of Mormon's messages and the
restoration of the gospel that there will
come for each of us a day in the not too
distant future when the air that we breathe
will be pungent with a heavenly ether that
is punctuated by the melodious strains of
our native language. Every detail will be
just as we had imagined it would be,
including our appreciation of the
reassuring radiant heat from
a celestial fire kindled
beforehand by our
Father.

We can turn to no-one but God for the heaven-sent assurances that liberate us from fear, doubt, the apprehension of danger, the turmoil of the world, and from the vagaries of men. Only when we have cast off the self-limiting conditions and the self-defeating behaviors that had blinded us to a larger view of life, will we be able to enjoy a settled conviction in our minds of the truthfulness of The Book of Mormon.

Again and again, we turn to The Book of Mormon, because none of us would purposely choose to become spiritually depleted, or to perish because we had willfully neglected the very things that matter the most. We understand that consequences inevitably follow doctrinal dehydration, spiritual starvation, and intellectual inhibition. Who could've guessed that a simple book (that is currently translated into 113 languages) could provide us with such powerful medicine?

As we think
about how The Book of
Mormon has touched our lives,
we respond to President Gordon B.
Hinckley's plea to do a little better, to be a
little more kind, to be a little more merciful,
and a little more forgiving; "to put behind us
our weaknesses of the past, and go forth with
new energy and increased resolution to
improve the world about us, whether it
be in our homes, in our places of
employment, or in our social
activities."

When we have completely immersed
ourselves in reading The Book of Mormon without
distraction, our thoughts will inevitably turn to the
Savior. We will feel His energy building within us,
lifting us to the zenith of experience where the lines
distinguishing mortality from heaven become
blurred. We will find ourselves consumed in
a fire of everlasting burnings, as we come
face to face with eternity through the
mighty influence of the Spirit
that can only come
from God.

All who've been
touched by the Spirit
as they study The Book
of Mormon realize that they
are the nobility of heaven, and
that they are rightful heirs of
a divine inheritance, and are
counted among those of a
choice and a chosen
generation. (See
1 Nephi 1:20).

When we've immersed ourselves in
our study of The Book of Mormon, we will
re-examine our priorities, enlarge our perceptions
to unleash a larger view of life, encourage the Spirit to
unlock our potential, and yield our will to God in order to
tap into His power. If, on the other hand, we've surrendered
our dreams to the narrow and confining reality of the carnal
and sensual world, we will suffer a defeat of cosmic proportion.
But if our behavior is in harmony with gospel principles, we will
find ourselves in a constant state of improvement leading to
perfection. In the process, we will be empowered to become
what we had heretofore scarcely dreamed possible. The
principles and doctrine of The Book of Mormon
will become the perfect law of liberty,
and its truth will set us free.
(See John 8:32).

Along
with our testimonies
of The Book of Mormon, we
will receive a variety of spiritual
gifts that, by themselves or taken
as a whole, can be the antidote for
the poisonous telestial tendencies
that suppress the expression of
God's celestial sureties.

The Book
of Mormon rivets
our attention upon our
witness of the Savior, which
the Spirit then encourages us
to nurture. Each time we pick up
the book and we take our testimony
temperature, we are able, once again,
to detect, and even augment, its
feverish pitch.

Angels from heaven will minister to our needs as a result of our engagement with The Book of Mormon. "For I will go before your face," said the Lord. "I will be on your right hand, and on your left, and my Spirit shall be in your hearts, and mine angels round about you, to bear you up." (D&C 84:88).

In The Book of Mormon, we are blessed with the opportunity to enjoy the best of both worlds; to live on the earth, to be sure, but also, to wrap our spirits around a reassuring message of peace surpassing our understanding.

When
we read The
Book of Mormon,
our guidance from the
Holy Ghost is the fruits
of the Spirit that we will
receive as we learn more
about the doctrine of
Christ.

As long as our priorities remain
out of order, coordinated with the world
but out of synch with heaven, we will lose
the power to bring about positive change in
our lives. The Book of Mormon will sharpen
our perspective, enabling us to comprehend
and build upon principles of perfection
that are validated by the Holy Ghost
and emulated by the example of
the Savior, Whose counsel is
the very centerpiece of
the text.

As our
lives conform to the
affable relationship that
should exist between ourselves
and the principles of The Book of
Mormon, we'll begin to understand
how covenants with God can help us to
overcome adversity to gain self-mastery.
We'll learn how God's promises can help
us to focus our efforts to become as He
is. With a quickening pulse, we'll
begin to see how its messages
can prepare us to live in
His presence.

In our moments of deepest
reflection, such as when we read
The Book of Mormon, we envision
"stepping on shore, and finding it
heaven! We visualize taking hold of
a hand, and finding it God's hand.
We dream of passing from storm
and tempest to an unbroken
calm, and of waking up,
and finding it home."
(Anonymous).

The word of God is
of such power that the law is
driven into our inward parts and
is written upon our hearts. A mighty
change takes place as we experience the
process of sanctification. When we are
born again, the desired result of all
gospel-oriented teaching has been
achieved, and we have no more
disposition to do evil, but to
do good continually. Our
faith is perfected as
we read The Book
of Mormon.

In the final analysis, our
righteous objective is to conduct
our lives in such a manner that the
Holy Ghost may justify us, and testify
that we have been perfectly obedient to our
covenants. This enables Heavenly Father
to welcome us into His Rest. His promised
blessings have the power to move us along
the path of progression to the point where
we will internalize His divine nature to
one day be comfortable when we find
ourselves kneeling before His throne.
This is a concept that is rehearsed
repetitively during our Book
Mormon study.

The sheer weight of our temporal baggage can create an imbalance in our lives that leads to confusion. The Book of Mormon jars us out of our collective complacency by upsetting the stagnation of the status quo. It invites us to enjoy a settled conviction in our minds by getting our juices flowing, prodding us to constructively expend our energy, and putting our agency to work. It compels us to be doers, to be actively engaged, and more than simply hearers. Those who've read the book tend to make things happen, while timid souls whose tentative steps can't quite lead them to testimony are doomed to ask, what happened.

The wide gulf that may seem to exist between saints and sinners does not matter much, for at the end of the day, how we respond to The Book of Mormon is the great equalizer. In its messages, we see how our Heavenly Father is no respecter of persons.

The raw, ugly, and festering sores that are manifestations of the infection of iniquity, that results from the contamination of sin, is incompatible with the uncompromising standard of spiritual hygiene that is required of all those who have a testimony of The Book of Mormon and hope to inhabit heaven, to live in the company of God and angels.

The merits of The Book of Mormon can be investigated only after we've nurtured a companionship with the Holy Ghost. When we fall under His spell, however, we will soon be at-one with the Savior of the world.

In
The Book
of Mormon, we
are oriented more
toward the expansive
laws of the eternal world
than we are to the restrictive
boundaries that are defined by
our physical surroundings. The
Spirit guides us to the physicality
of heartfelt repentance, and to our
expanding comprehension of the
otherworldly doctrine found in
the Atonement. The Plan of
God bridges both time
and space.

The Book
of Mormon
can catalyze
our relationship
with God, when it
unshackles us from
the chilly grip of our
captivity to Satan.
All is because of
the Atonement
of Christ.

When we read The Book of Mormon, we experience sensations of serenity and harmony, in ways that have been thoughtfully designed by our Heavenly Father to touch our heart strings. These inner stirrings defy any rational explanation.

There is an ever-present negative energy influencing every action, and The Book of Mormon is our potent countermeasure. Its sole stipulations are that we confess if we've embraced the opposites that lie before us, and that we immediately undertake the safety protocols required by repentance to bring us back to a state of accord with heaven.

Lucifer fell from heaven with a resoundingly deafening thud, and we feel the reverberations of its after-shocks even today, when we decline the invitation to read and pray about The Book of Mormon.

Our spiritual renewal through the Sacrament doesn't give us license to act recklessly, or to be drawn, even intermittently, to the Dark Side, to sample the pleasures of Babylon, or to neglect our consistent study of The Book of Mormon.

Yielding to
the enticements of the
Devil leaves us gasping for
a quick breath of the celestial
air that can only be found in the
ventilation systems that service the
sanctuaries where we go to study the
gospel and The Book of Mormon. It is
there where we will find shelter from
the choking sandstorms of sin that
continually rake across the barren
desert wastes of Babylon.

If we hope to successfully
deal with the inequalities of
life and escape the quicksands
of self-pity, we must personalize
the lessons of the Atonement, and
that can be best accomplished as
we familiarize ourselves with
the Doctrine of Christ that
is found in 2 Nephi
Chapter 31.

Those who are
of a weak will, whose
secret gardens of wheat,
the staff of life, have become
infested with tares, and who have
then lost their desire to examine the
virtues of The Book of Mormon, have
simply exchanged the blessings of heaven
and earth for the provocative pleasures that
are provided by the pandering purveyor of
poor choices. They quickly become snared
by the Devil and are bound by his strong
chains. Too late, they realize that their
misguided loyalty has limited their
options, restricted their actions,
fettered their self-expression,
and shut the door on the
guiding influence of
the Spirit.

The Book
of Mormon blesses
us with the capacity to
reach out to touch the face
of God with an incorruptible
and unimpeachable spiritual
sixth sense that finds its
expression deep inside
us, within our own
hearts.

The
unrepentant
are argumentive;
abuse their position,
and exercise unrighteous
dominion, whereas those who
are driven by the principles found
in The Book of Mormon speak softly,
seek peaceful solutions to their problems,
invite the Spirit to guide them, and learn
to let the love of God and others be the
engine that drives their behavior.

Jalal al Din
al Rumi, the 14th century
Sufi poet who founded the Order
of Dervishes, wrote: "When we are dead,
others will seek our tomb not in the earth,
but will find it in the hearts of men." It is
within our hearts that we have determined to
receive The Book of Mormon, and we are broken
down with humility as we receive chastisement
and counsel from the Lord and His servants.
We forgive those who may have offended us,
and we render service to others. Our good
example teaches them that blessings
will follow when find out what
Jesus would have us do,
and we do it!

Habitual sin can act as a quicksand that will mire the unwary in a monotonously repetitive and underwhelming convention and a mind-numbing conformity. These are the opposites of the imaginative spontaneity and the refreshingly distinctive artistic individuality found in all who enjoy the Spirit through their internalization of the principles that may be found in The Book of Mormon.

We can infer from the casualty count following the ideological War in Heaven, that some of our Father in Heaven's children have forfeit their opportunity to obtain a body. (See 2 Nephi Chapter 24). For those who remained faithful in the pre-earth existence, however, there have come humbling liabilities; thus, the Plan required our Heavenly Father to recreate the order of heaven in The Book of Mormon, that we might have a tool to regularly recalibrate our sights on the glory of our former home. Thereby, the book has become a beacon of light for the weary in a lone and dreary world.

Directly opposite the path to Calvary is the road to self-indulgence; the opposite of our submission to the will of God is self-gratification; the opposite of our reverential worship during our study of The Book of Mormon is idolatry. It is that plain and simple.

God knows what is best for His children, and He has confidence in our divine potential to acquire His nature. He commands us develop faith, to repent, to be baptized, and He invites the Spirit to guide us to these goals that lie easily within our reach and that have been spelled out with precision in The Book of Mormon. Its principles and doctrine become the foundation of the requirements that must be met if we hope to gain readmittance to the Kingdom of God.

In The
Book of Mormon,
we are taught that it
is in our nature to make
mistakes and to learn from
them, but it's also in our DNA
to want to grasp the horns of
sanctuary, so that at the end
of the day we may still be
justified by the grace
of God.

The Book of
Mormon inspires the
disciples of Christ to help
their less fortunate brethren
"to bear their weaknesses, to be
courteous unto them, to win them
unto Christ, and to overcome them
with kindness." (William Tyndall).
They are always ready to give courage
and hope, and to speak kind words that
awaken the souls of others to cheeriness,
"until hearts meet with hearts and rejoice
in friendship that ever is true." ("Let Us
Oft Speak Kind Words"). Their charity
is founded upon forgiveness, triggered
by tolerance, affected by appreciation,
and reflected in respect. Their kind
words are as keys that unlock
the gates of heaven.

Agency and opposition are always before us, and The Book of Mormon stands as a sacred sentinel, inviting us to enter in at heaven's gate, to find the Rest of God.

The Devil will tempt us to tarry on detours from The Book of Mormon that will transport us into telestial traffic jams, religious roundabout, and doctrinal dead ends, from which the only escape is repentance.

The Book of
Mormon teaches us that
repentance is made possible
by the Atonement. It, and the
Sacrament, remove the stain
of sin from the tapestry
that is the tableau
of our lives.

The Book of
Mormon teaches that the
Sacrament, together with the
Atonement of Jesus Christ, makes
life eternal, love immortal, and
death but a horizon which is
nothing, save the limit
of our sight.

No matter how ponderous the impediments may be that result from inattention to our spiritual well-being, The Book of Mormon teaches that after our purposeful repentance, the Atonement, by the power of the Spirit, will lift us up at the last day. (See Alma 36:3).

Sadly, The Book of Mormon repeatedly illustrates how sinful behavior might appear to be the latest in fashion to the worldly-wise. But it also demonstrates that the styles that are popular today won't wear so well in heaven, whose dress code abhors iniquity. Its standards are clearly spelled out in the scriptures. In short, when choosing our spiritual wardrobe, it is a good rule of thumb is to remember that unrighteousness is never a good look. (See 2 Nephi 8:24).

The Book of Mormon provides us with all the tools we'll need to recalibrate our spiritual appestats when we notice they're not in synch with the principles of the gospel, and we find ourselves indulging, or worse yet, binge eating, in sin, which we'd never before supposed could happen.

The neglect of our spiritual welfare requires us to take drastic action. Intensive care primarily consisting of Book of Mormon doctrine will become necessary if we hope to experience a reversal of our fortunes and if, when the bandages finally come off, we think we will look in the mirror and see in our countenances the image and likeness of God.

The Book of Mormon shows us how to increase our metaphysical metabolism, to burn away as much of the fat of faithlessness as we can, that our hearts might be broken and melt in the heat of the crucible of contrition.

Our salvation has not so much to do with cherubim and a flaming sword as it does with how we feel about The Book of Mormon, and how we act upon those feelings.

Because there exist no dry cleaning solvents to apply to the stains of sin, The Book of Mormon teaches that we will remain unclean in the sight of God for as long as we refuse the healing waters of baptism, or if we thereafter rebuff the invitation of God to continually repent and seek His forgiveness for our transgressions.

The Book of Mormon teaches us that the Atonement is the best fire insurance policy that could ever be issued, for it is underwritten by God, indemnifying us against being burned as stubble at the Rapture. (See 3 Nephi 25:1 & 1 Thessalonians 4:15-17). If we have faithfully paid our premiums on time and in the sum of a broken heart and contrite spirit, we'll receive full value (as well as a full refund!) on the day of Judgment. We will inherit immortal bodies in the resurrection, certified to not only withstand, but also to thrive, within the everlasting burnings of the Kingdom of God. (See D&C 121:11).

When the
Nephites were
at their best, their
craving to be clean
found expression in
celestial sparks that
ignited their desire
to continually
repent.

The faith
of the Nephites
was dormant without
the accompanying work
of repentance that was made
possible by the Atonement and
that was repetitively invigorated by
their participation in the Sacrament.
Nonetheless, their faith alone could not
produce the requisite power to save them
from the unalterable demands of Justice.
That Mercy might prevail, covenants and
their related ordinances were inaugurated
to focus their attention on the Law of the
Gospel, the Law of Sacrifice, the Law
of Consecration, and the Savior's
Atonement.

We recall how the Ghostbusters were slimed when they engaged the power of Gozer the Destructor in New York City, but the Nephite children to whom the Savior ministered during His post-mortal ministry in another part of His vineyard were destined, instead, to be showered in stardust and covered with the glitter of the Gods, as they rubbed shoulders with His angels who came down from heaven to minister among them.

The Nephites were nurtured within a generous culture medium of faith, validated by baptism in a metaphysical reunion with God. It was witnessed in the fiery cauldron of the Spirit, and in the only way possible to ransom them from their sins and keep them on a strait and narrow way.

The Last
Days are muddled by
competing voices that threaten
to get in the way of the revelation
that is meant to be received when we read
The Book of Mormon. (See Moroni 7:12-13).
Its companion feelings of insight, intuition,
and inspiration are fundamental and intrinsic
to the recognition of the principles and doctrines, to
the successful execution of the ordinances, and to the
purposeful implementation of each covenant that is
related to the Plan of Salvation. These emotions
will stand out in sharp contrast to the gross
darkness that so frequently shrouds the
minds of the ignorant. (See D&C
112:23, & Isaiah 29:18).

Ever since the
Fall of Adam and Eve,
Satan has utilized a free pass
to mingle among the sons and
daughters of God on the earth. This
flushes him with excitement, because he
knows how difficult it is for us to resist
our natural tendency toward volatility
that neutralizes the spirit of revelation
that is found in The Book of Mormon.
Those who love Satan more than they
love God unavoidably exhibit the
behavioral manifestations of
that misplaced adoration,
as they walk in the
dark, the blind
leading the
blind.

John F. Kennedy famously declared: "We choose to do things, not because they are easy but because they are hard. It is our goals that organize and measure the output of our energies and skills. Our challenges are those that we are willing to accept, that we are unwilling to postpone, but that we intend to win." That is well put, but we must never forget that one plus God equals a majority. We need to keep the focus of our faith on the Savior of whom The Book of Mormon testifies, so that when we are figuratively tapped on the shoulder to accomplish special things, we will be both prepared and qualified through the grace of God for what could be our finest hour.

If we hunger and thirst after a comprehension of true principles, and come to the Savior anticipating a spiritual feast, the doctrine and principles of The Book of Mormon will distill upon our souls as the dews of heaven, the Holy Ghost will be our constant companion, and by the power of revelation we may discern the truth of all things.

As one
would expect,
The Book of Mormon
nurtures our relationship
with God and the Holy Ghost.
We become the fashioners of our
fortunes as we learn to rely upon
reserves that are only found in
our Savior, Jesus Christ. We
realize that His wisdom is
infinitely greater than
our understanding
of anything and
everything.

As we ponder
the messages from
The Book of Mormon,
all that we must do will be
revealed to us in spectacular
simplicity and plainness. The
Spirit will comfort and succor
us with the bread of life. As we
journey through the harsh and
unforgiving environment of
Idumea, seeking our Savior
while He may be found, an
oasis will spring up in
the desert of life, and
His living water
will slake our
thirst.

It is only through the
uninterrupted attention of,
and intervention by, our Father
in Heaven, His Son Jesus Christ,
and the Holy Ghost, that mortality
can become the wonderful revelatory
learning center for the talented and
gifted that it was envisioned to be
even before the world was made.
For surely the Lord God will
do nothing, except He reveal
(in The Book of Mormon)
His secret to those whom
the faithful esteem as
His prophets and
seers.

Revelation works its
magic to forge a spiritual
connection between ourselves
and our fellow travelers, and our
Heavenly Father, by our obedience
to His laws that are more expansive
than any carnal commandments
could ever be. To be fulfilled, they
require the fulness of the gospel,
that is to say, the principles
and the doctrine that are
found in The Book
of Mormon.

A spectacular panorama is unfolding right before our eyes because of The Book of Mormon. If we want to gain a testimony of the divinity of Jesus Christ, nativity scenes may encourage us, carols may prompt us, and gift-giving may put us in the mood, but we receive His sure witness in dreams and visions, by voices, promptings, a burning in the bosom, and in strokes of inspiration. "For God speaketh once, yea twice, yet man perceiveth it not. In a dream, in a vision of the night, when deep sleep falleth upon men, in slumberings upon the bed; then he openeth the ears of men, and sealeth their instruction." (Job 33:14-16).

In his Introduction to The Book of Mormon, Joseph Smith declared that it was "the most correct of any book on earth and the keystone of our religion, and (that we would) get nearer to God by abiding by its precepts, than by any other book." It will influence us to be more trusting and to speak without guile; to be more transparent and less prejudicial; to have fewer pretensions and to be more genuine; slower to judgment and quicker to forgive. It's teachings will motivate us to greet others with a warm "Hello Neighbor!" as did Mr. Rogers.

The Book of Mormon will help us to focus on what God wants to happen, instead of allowing ourselves to be distracted by what we don't want to happen. Revelation shows us how to envision success so that the conclusion will be foregone. It sends out a reassuring message to every child of God that their fondest dreams will come true, and that in a coming day they will enjoy a dance with Deity beneath the reassuring glow of the stars of heaven. But more than that, it outlines the way for them to keep that date with their destiny.

The Book of Mormon enlightens our understanding, that we might embrace the hope of the high calling of our Savior Jesus Christ, and that the riches of glory might abide, through the grace of God, as our unmerited inheritance.

Those who freely
allow themselves to be
bound by revelation take
commitment to a whole new
level. They redefine dedication.
They exercise their duties in ways
that are truly selfless. The gospel has
transformed their lives. They are as the
people of Zarahemla, who proclaimed to
King Benjamin: "The Spirit of the Lord
Omnipotent ..... has wrought a mighty
change in us, or in our hearts, that we
have no more disposition to do evil,
but to do good continually."
(Mosiah 5:2).

When
we have The
Book of Mormon
to guide us, we know
how to worship, and we
know what to worship, for
truth may be recognized by
its effects. The way to test the
claims made by the gospel of
Jesus Christ is by rendering
our unswerving obedience
to its principles of
action.

The messianic prophet Isaiah wrote: "For unto us
a child is born; unto us a son is given." (Isaiah 9:6) Our
testimony of The Book of Mormon, that stands as a witness to the
birth of the holy child, and of the Mighty God, the Everlasting Father,
and the Prince of Peace, is also 'borne.' In the initial stages of our spiritual
awakening, our testimony is born in the classical sense, with physical and
emotional struggle. It is born of foundation faith in Jesus Christ and the
principles of the gospel. Then, we bear our testimony by carrying it
with us at all times. We also bear our testimony as we give it to
others because we are perpetually thrilled with life, are
possessed by the Spirit, and want to share our
enjoyment of celestial inspiration.

It is by our faith
in the revealed word of
The Book of Mormon that we
commit ourselves to the arduous
process of a spiritual rebirth that
accompanies our choice of life and
light. To neglect to do so would be a
capitulation to a miscarriage that is
personified by death and darkness.
That resulting fear can be character
crippling. It can be devastating to
the capacity of our listening ears
to be able to recognize truth as
the Holy Ghost speaks to us
by power of heaven.

If we will read, study, and pray about it with care, we will discover how Book of Mormon prophets encouraged their people to have lips that articulate nothing but uplifting expressions that would never speak guile, and shoulders that have developed the strength to bear the burdens of those who have been battered and bruised by the vicissitudes of life and who may be faltering under the heavy weight of sorrow, or of unresolved sin.

Those with faith will hunger and thirst after righteousness. They will be filled with the spirit of revelation and will love The Book of Mormon. They will press forward with dedication, and will feast on the scriptures. They will receive physical and spiritual nourishment, and will endure throughout mortality with continuing responsibility, and with the accountability that accompanies obedience to all of the laws of God.

As we fine-tune our revelatory capabilities, we can build upon experiences with the Holy Ghost that we have already had, that have come to us as we've patiently waited upon the Lord. These include our testimonies of Jesus Christ and of His gospel, of the divine nature of The Book of Mormon, and of the mission of the prophet Joseph Smith.

Its easy to talk about revelation in shallow ways, by retreating into insipid and colorless verbiage as the easy way out. And so, we take care to avoid steering a course that would take us away from The Book of Mormon with inconsiderate, dismissive, or offhand expressions.

Jesus
encourages us
to give of ourselves
completely and without
reservation, so that we might
enjoy a state of harmony with
Him and synchronization with
the heavens. He asks us to search
without ceasing in our quest to
discover within The Book of
Mormon the divine center
of our faith.

Those of us
who have the faith to
become the beneficiaries
of the blessings of The Book
of Mormon have been touched by
angels who walk with us along
paths that are illuminated by
the stunning light of
the Lord.

Today our society, which is arguably good, has nevertheless utterly failed to instill within the rising generation any significant appreciation of the revelatory capacity of God. When a culture is led to believe that truth is relative or that the merits of faith can be arbitrarily determined without the need for the intervention of heaven, such as is documented in The Book of Mormon, the stage will have been set for a disaster of biblical proportion.

Our Father in Heaven is bursting with excitement to reveal many important things that pertain to His Kingdom. He sends us tenderly composed letters of encouragement, such as those that can be found in The Book of Mormon, hoping that we will receive and read them with enthusiasm. Lines of communication from the Spirit are nurtured to become broad avenues of correspondence freely flowing back and forth between the heavens and the earth.

The world
seeks to change us by
exerting external controls,
but it has failed miserably in
its attempts to do so. The Savior
makes change by transforming
the inner vessel, and He succeeds
brilliantly. He goes about doing
this by calibrating our internal
sextants, so that we may take
our bearings on the guiding
stars of revelations from
the heavens, such as
can be found in
The Book of
Mormon.

Every time we think in
rational terms, we risk being
hedged in by the very things from
which we yearn to be free: our mortal
perspective and perceptions, that are, sad
'tho it may be, the sum and substance of our
temporal experiences. Because of the Light of
Christ, we're all intuitively drawn to seek the
right answers, but if we haven't also received
revelation such as is found in The Book of
Mormon, which is the further light and
knowledge that the Lord has promised
to give to us (see D&C 50:24), we'll
be at risk of asking the wrong
questions, and to do so
habitually.

Some have embraced the merits of The Book of Mormon because they have discovered that it is only by establishing communication with God that we receive transfusions of the spiritual element. It is as a heavenly dialysis machine, where worldly contaminants are removed from our systems because we are incapable of accomplishing the task on our own. The resources we need are only to be found in the correspondence that exists between ourselves and the heavens.

Read yourselves full, think yourselves straight, pray yourselves hot, and let yourselves go! The first three of these admonitions involve faithful preparation. They set the stage for purposeful action, to 'let ourselves go' as we listen for the peaceful, revelatory counsel of the Spirit that is found in The Book of Mormon.

We read in The Book
of Mormon that peace on earth
and good will toward others actually
has a pretty good chance of eventually
becoming a reality. As we look around at
a world that's gone mad, the book provides a
refuge from the uncertainties of life. To those
who are unsure, tentative, and hesitant,
it speaks a language of stability,
direction, and purpose.

The Lord selects those
who are meek and humble, and then,
He tutors them thru the Light of Christ, the
power of the Holy Ghost, and the influence of
The Book of Mormon. Those whom He selects are
"the weak things of the world." (D&C 1:19). As
President Kimball once stated: "Christianity
did not go from Rome to Galilee. It was
the other way around. In our day,
the routing is from Palmyra
to Paris, and not the
reverse."

When we enjoy
a rapport with the Spirit,
our faith to act will generate
the power to do God's will in an
expansive and interactive way,
in holiness. We will recognize
His revelatory voice found in
The Book of Mormon, which
"abideth and hath no end.
And if it be in (us) it
shall abound."
(D&C 88:66).

Those blessed with
testimonies of The Book of
Mormon will find the strength to
break free of "the influence of that
spirit which hath so strongly riveted
the creeds of the fathers, who have
inherited lies, upon the hearts of
the children, and filled the
world with confusion.
(D&C 123:7).

Even
with light
from The Book
of Mormon, we only
dimly perceive our noble
heritage, and we sometimes
find it difficult to accept the fact
that we mingled among the Gods
before our mortal births. The Hubble
telescope can 'see' 13.2 billion light
years into our past, almost back to
the moment of creation itself, but
it cannot gaze into heaven for
five minutes. Nothing but
the revelation of God has
the capacity to do
that.

The Book
of Mormon is like a
star map created by the
hand of God to illuminate
the pathway to the promised
land. Only His endowment of
the unearthly power of radiant
light has the capacity to disperse
the darkness from before us, and
to cause the heavens to shake for
our good. (See D&C 21:6).

In the Book of Mormon, we quickly learn to respond to God's heavenly smile that has been cleverly disguised as revelation, so that one day, we might be asked to participate in our own celestial inner beauty contest.

Blind opposition, enmity, hatred, hostility, inflexibility, and intolerance are the angry manifestations of pride, but these are overwhelmed by the faith, hope, and charity of those who have learned to respond to the revelatory promptings found in The Book of Mormon.

The 30-year-old Prophet Joseph Smith had only recently completed his translation of The Book of Mormon when he prayed: "Help us by the power of thy Spirit, that we may mingle our voices with those bright, shining seraphs around thy throne, with acclimations of praise, singing Hosanna to God and the Lamb!" (D&C 109:79).

It is the reality of of revelation that gives us the courage to "try the virtue of the word of God." (Alma 31:5). We do so, that we might reap its rewards, and then, with diligence, patience, faith, and long-suffering, harvest the fruit of the Tree of Life from its low hanging branches.

Joseph Smith taught that "we may profit by noticing the first intimation of the spirit of revelation; for instance, when we feel pure intelligence flowing into us, it may give us sudden strokes of ideas ... By learning the Spirit of God and understanding it, we may grow into the principle of revelation." The Holy Ghost, then, is our schoolmaster Who is commissioned to bring us, through the doctrine of Christ found in The Book of Mormon, into the hallowed halls of direct communication with Deity.

The truthfulness of the doctrine and principles that have been incorporated into the text of The Book of Mormon may be recognized only if we've fallen under the influence of the Spirit. Communication from the heavens only waits upon our initiative. So it is with the covenants and ordinances of the gospel. They remain virtually untouched by private interpretation. In a perfect storm of our knowledge, belief, and faith, it is the sunlight of revelation that will turn on as a bright and shining star in the heavens, that is energized by the inexhaustible fuel of a chain reaction within a celestial reactor.

Our faith
is a tool that
allows us to see
beyond the limited
horizon of our sight,
to be touched by a vision
of the virtue of the word of
God as it has been revealed in
The Book of Mormon. We savor
the truth with a discriminating
taste that allows us to discern
the distinctive flavor of
eternal worlds.

Without The Book of
Mormon, it would be much
harder for us to acknowledge the
revelatory autobiographical thread
that wends its way from heaven to the
earth. Sometimes, we can't see the forest
for the trees, and we forget that "trailing
clouds of glory have we come from our
God, Who is our Home." (William
Wordsworth).

The Book of
Mormon provides many
of the threads that have gone
into a fabric that has then been
fashioned into a tapestry that is a
celebration of our lives. We basically
turn to the inventory of yarn that God
has provided for us in a continual stream
of vibrant colors. With these, He empowers
us to weave imaginative new patterns that
will inevitably become a reflection of our
confidence in the creativity of His
overall Plan.

The Book of Mormon
reintroduces us to the quiet
instruction from our Heavenly
Father that sustained us during
the spiritual kindergarten years of
our pre-mortal existence. Once again,
we are blessed to walk in the light of
the Lord, and return in our hearts
to that more comfortable state of
harmony with which we were
so familiar in the secret
gardens of our
youth.

The Book of Mormon may be the closest thing that we'll ever have to a perpetual motion machine, inasmuch as for nearly two hundred years, without interruption, it's been propelling the Saints along on their passage heavenward. But we mustn't become too comfortable with it, for "our Father in Heaven refreshes us on the journey through life with some pleasant inns, but he will not encourage us to mistake them for home." (C.S. Lewis).

We learn from the Book of Mormon that the powers of heaven cannot be handled nor controlled except upon the basis of righteousness that is not superficial or ritualistic. When "the Pharisees were gathered together, Jesus asked them, Saying, What think ye of Christ? Whose son is he?" Sadly, their sluggish response, "The Son of David," was tendered with little feeling or emotion. (Matthew 22:41-42). Although it was technically correct, it lacked spiritual horsepower. Its dearth of traction was obvious, its inability to generate spontaneity was palpable, its lack of energy to engage enthusiasm was noticeable, its incapacity to spark vitality was evident, and its abject failure to candidly acknowledge the powerful relationship that can exist between ourselves and God was clear. Our own responses to the Lord's penetrating questions must arise out of deeper convictions.

Once we've internalized the Book of Mormon's teachings relating to doctrine and principles, we will find that we are more comfortable responding to the question: Whom say ye that I am?" as was Peter. Without even a moment's hesitation, the Lord's faithful disciple declared: "Thou art the Christ, the Son of the Living God."
(Matthew 16:15-16).

Because of The Book of Mormon, borders are opened, every requirement of citizenship is waived, and all the world is invited to partake of the blessings that freely flow out of the little town of Bethlehem.

The Book of Mormon makes it easier for the gospel to be taken into the world, but it never works out so well when it's the other way around.

The Book of Mormon remains the sole possession of a peculiar people. This is as it should be, because "it would be impossible for us to become popular with the world, because then all hell would want to join us." (Ezra Taft Benson).

We infer from The Book of Mormon that we ought to be satisfied with our circumstances and at peace with our lot in life; that we should be grateful for what we have been given, rather than frustrated because of what we have been denied.

The real gifts of the restoration of the gospel that flow from the principles and doctrine that are explained in The Book of Mormon include baptism (a covenant of salvation), the companionship of the Holy Ghost (a covenant of justification), the Sacrament (a covenant of sanctification), and celestial marriage (a covenant of exaltation).

It is only necessary to pay the equitable price of a broken heart and a contrite spirit to discover the merits of The Book of Mormons' treasures and the relevance of its messages. These include a wealth of doctrine imbedded in a historical matrix that touches on reality in a thousand different ways. It has permitted the restoration to move forward and the church to be organized. It has given us the gift of a fifth Gospel (3 Nephi), that summarizes the ministry of Christ in the New World. It fulfilled the prophecies of Ezekiel and Isaiah. It has empowered church members to stand out prominently among their Christian neighbors, and it has endowed them with an element of singularity that distinguishes them from other denominations, allowing the line in the sand separating the faithful from the world to be more clearly defined.

When we delve into The Book of Mormon, we learn about Zion and adopt its substantive lifestyle, in contrast to Babylon's transparency. We have learned to trust in Zion's grip on reality even as Babylon grasps for straws in the confusion of an illusion that is of its own making. We know that Zion will deal in spiritual absolutes even as Babylon tosses to and fro in a vacuum of moral relativism. We have witnessed the focus of Zion, as well as Babylon's congenital spiritual short-sightedness. We are comforted that Zion is grounded on the bedrock of principles, and we see how Babylon only basks in a false sense of security, mistaking its values for principles, while erroneously thinking that all is well, even as the world comes crashing down around its ears.

How quickly are we "lifted up in pride; yea, how quick to boast." (Helaman 12:5). And yet, how great an example were the Wise Men of the East. They may have been the Magi of Zoroastrianism, wearing the trappings of wealth, enjoying position, and bearing costly gifts, but it was their humility that constrained them to make the arduous journey from the East all the way to Bethlehem. It is significant that over 2,000 years later, we still hold them in great esteem, and refer to them as "Wise Men."

Ultimately, the hours that we devote to the study of The Book of Mormon is time well-spent. It is a time of rebirth, renewal, and rededication. God has revealed His Plan because our perspective needs to be crystal clear so we can concentrate on the principles of perfection that are validated by the Spirit, fueled by the power of His priesthood, and revealed and restored by legal administrators that have been sent from heaven.

About fifteen million people in the world die from starvation each year. That's one person every 2.1 seconds. Currently, while around 146,000 people die each day (about 100 a minute) only about 250,000 eternal lives are saved each year (about 1 every 2 minutes) because they have been protected from spiritual malnutrition by The Book of Mormon as they have been taught the principles of the gospel. This number has remained relatively steady for many years. If we did it the Lord's way, however, the world could be saved in 10 years; say, 5 million this year, and 10 million next year, 20 million the next year, 40 million the following year, and so on, until in the 10th year, over 8.6 billion of our Heavenly Father's children would have been taught about the Plan of Salvation, if each member would share his or her testimony with one just other person during each of those years. There is more than enough spiritual food to go around, to feed every person on earth.

There are three elements of teaching that relate to the core curriculum of The Book of Mormon. They are 1) teach key doctrine, 2) extend an invitation to action, and 3) describe promised blessings. Thomas S. Monson offered this counsel: "The goal of gospel teaching," he said, 'is not to pour information into the minds of class members. Its aim is to inspire the individual to think about, feel about, and then do something about living gospel principles."

Our capacity to absorb the teachings that are found in The Book of Mormon is energized by our intrinsic sense of nobility, for we are the sons and daughters of a King. In France during the Middle Ages, the successor to the throne of the Bourbon monarchs was known as the Dauphin. During the reign of his father, unscrupulous and crafty counselors tried every means to corrupt the Dauphin, to thereby make him ineligible to inherit the throne. In all of their attempts, however, they were unsuccessful. Finally, in resignation, they asked him: "How is it that with all of our enticements we have not been able to compromise your high standards?" His reply was simple: "I am a King's son." The Dauphin had established behavior patterns that were consistent with his beliefs, and that was what allowed him to act and to move forward in perfect harmony with his convictions.

When we take the plunge into The Book of Mormon and we find ourselves immersed in its teachings, the quiet whisperings of the Spirit reassure us that "surely, whoever speaks to me in the right voice, him or her I shall follow, as the waters follow the moon, silently and with fluid steps, anywhere around the globe." (Walt Whitman).

In The Book of Mormon, we learn about the reaffirmation of the promise of a God-centered earth that is "full of the knowledge of the Lord, as the waters cover the sea." (2 Nephi 21:9, see Isaiah 11:9). "No form of government, no level of material well-being, will save us. We will be redeemed only when towers fall and Bethlehem triumphs over Babylon. What is at stake, finally, is not only intelligence, but also feeling. We have to change our hearts."
(Abba Eban).

Nephi clearly taught that "it is by grace that we are saved, after all we can do." (2 Nephi 25:23). Latter-day Saints, however, have the tendency to emphasize works to the point that it may seem to others that the grace of God takes a back seat to their own efforts to earn salvation. In spite of their focus on industry, agency, accountability, and labor, as they are exhorted to greater dedication, diligence, and duty, the truth is that nothing we can do will ever qualify us to enjoy eternal life. Paul echoed Nephi, writing that it is "by grace (we) are saved, through faith, and that not of (our)selves. It is the gift of God."
(Ephesians 2:8).

Valiant souls who are firm in their faith and believe that The Book of Mormon is yet Another Testament of Jesus Christ, will find that heave will come knocking at their door. When it does, they will get up and open it.

At their best, the Nephites viewed the commandments as a consummate compilation of affirmative actions, and they were committed by covenant to a lifestyle that was centered on Christ. Members of His church found that the relationship between the commandments and blessings were directly proportional. They realized it is practically impossible to have one without the other. It was only this perspective that makes sense of the Savior's reassurance that His yoke is easy and His burden is light. It is little wonder that this message has been interpreted as the gospel of repentance and that we're encouraged to rely upon His merits that are crowned by the greatest blessing of all, which is that of His infinite and eternal Atonement for our sins.

The Holy Ghost certainly knows how, but instead He patiently shows how. Even though the devil has street smarts, the Lord has reassured us that priesthood-directed training and in-service is a better delegation of responsibility. He said of those who sought to destroy the work of the publication of The Book of Mormon: "I will show unto them that my wisdom is greater than the cunning of the devil." (D&C 10:43). In fact, He has a perfect way to detect the fingerprints of Satan: "I show unto you the way to judge; for every thing which inviteth to do good, and to persuade to believe in Christ, is sent forth by the power and gift of Christ; wherefore ye may know with a perfect knowledge it is of God." (Moroni 7:16).

We quickly learn, as we read The Book of Mormon, that the Holy Ghost doesn't have a pronoun problem. He doesn't say "I"; instead, He says "We." I and mine are usually accompanied by the unbended knee. The Savior spoke of our potential that stems from interdependency, when He said that we may "become the sons of God, even one in me as I am one in the Father, as the Father is one in me, that we may be one." (D&C 35:2). In contrast, we read the account of Lucifer, who had a pronoun problem of monumental proportion. As Isaiah wrote: "How art thou fallen from heaven, O Lucifer, son of the morning! How art thou cut down to the ground, which didst weaken the nations! For thou hast said in thine heart, I will ascend into heaven, I will exalt my throne above the stars of God: I will sit also upon the mount of the congregation, in the sides of the north: I will ascend above the heights of the clouds; I will be like the most High." (Isaiah 14:12-14)

Among the Nephites, it was their faith that set them free from the self-defeating behaviors of confusion, doubt, ignorance, sin, worry, and guilt, that might have caused them to become immobilized, and even paralyzed, during their mortal experience. It was in a garden setting that Adam and Eve were blessed with freedom to act, but the Nephites sometimes forfeit that birthright thru the adoption of bad habits. They were detained by telestial traffic jams, confused by conceptual cul-de-sacs, and detoured by doctrinal dilemmas of their own making. When they embarked upon the strait and narrow way, however, they found a path opening up onto the broad boulevards of opportunity that led to the perfect law of liberty, and to an expression of mind, body, and spirit that guided them toward the surety that is described in the scriptures as the Rest of the Lord. (See Alma 7:27).

When our minds are locked on terrestrial targets and we even attempt so-called higher-level thinking as we study The Book of Mormon, without the influence of the Spirit, we risk becoming as sounding brass and tinkling cymbals. Without the Holy Ghost's guidance, we will be hollow on the inside, and the echoes of silence will be deafening to our ears.

For latter-day apostate Nephites and Lamanites, the concept of the Atonement may be hard to grasp because it was conceived in heaven. It is not of this world, and if we try to wrap our finite minds around it, we will fail to do so. It can only be spiritually discerned.

Jacob addressed all of those who gun their engines in telestial traffic jams, become hoarders of temporal trash, and who have a fascination with trivial pursuits: "Wo unto him...that wasteth the days of his probation, for awful is his state!" (2 Nephi 9:27). Particularly when individuals groan "under darkness and under the bondage of sin," they have no hope, and their lives have little meaning or stability. (D&C 84:49). They cannot begin to comprehend that fame is a vapor, and popularity is an accident, and those who cheer you today might curse you tomorrow; that, in the end, the only thing that endures, the only thing that you can really count on, is your character. And that is something upon which you cannot put a price.

Commentary, Compendia, & Observations Index

the process of
our investigation of
The Book of Mormon, our
mystical relationship with God
is etched into our spiritual identity.
We become perfect in our faith as we make
a connection with Deity. That is how members
of The Church of Jesus Christ of Latter-day Saints
have the presumption to declare that it is our destiny
to rule as kings and queens, priests and priestesses, in
the house of Israel forever, and to reign with authority over
kingdoms, thrones, principalities, powers, dominions, and
exaltations. That will happen only when our connection to
God has matured to such magnitude and strength that our
identities become indistinguishable from each other. That
can only occur when we have received both His image
and His likeness in our countenances in the process
of a mind-bending spiritual metamorphosis. And
it is revelation from God that facilitates
that transformation.

Commentary Volume One
Born in The Wilderness

- 1 Nephi
- 2 Nephi
- Jacob
- Enos
- Jarom
- Omni
- Words of Mormon
- Observations
- Author's Note
- Addendum – A Sampling of Scriptures

Commentary Volume Two
Voices From The Dust

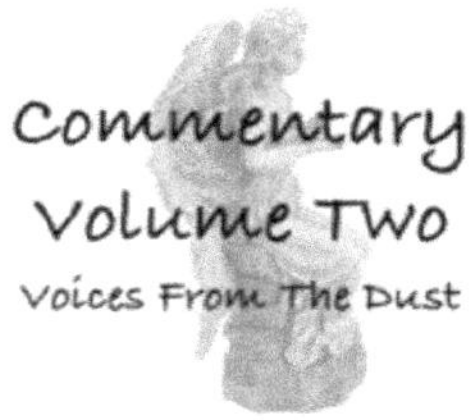

- Mosiah
- Alma
- Observations
- Author's Note
- Addendum – A Sampling of Scriptures

Commentary Volume Three
Journey to Cumorah

- Helaman
- 3 Nephi
- 4 Nephi
- Mormon
- Ether
- Moroni
- Observations
- Author's Note
- Addendum – A Sampling of Scriptures

The Book of Mormon has the depth, breadth, majesty, and capacity to encircle all of God's children within its tender embrace.

Compendium
Volume One

- Introduction
- Questions Answered by The Book of Mormon
- Topical Index
- Observations
- A few of my favorite things
- Familiar Scriptures
- Commentary & Compendium Index

Compendium
Volume Two

- Introduction
- Questions Answered by The Book of Mormon
- Topical Index
- Without The Book of Mormon
- Observations
- Introduction to the Isaiah Chapters
- "And it came to pass in The Book of Mormon
- "Ad thus we see" in The Book of Mormon
- "Behold" in The Book of Mormon
- "Wherefore" and "Therefore in The Book of Mormon
- The Appearance of Gold
- The Use of The Name of Christ
- Pragmatism in The Book of Mormon
- Dry Humor in The Book of Mormon
- A Book of Mormon Timeline
- Commentary and Compendium Index

Compendium
Volume Three

- Compendia Index
- Essays That Relate to Teachings in The Book of Mormon
- Observations
- Commentary, Compendium, & Observations Index

Compendium
Volume Four

- Compendia Index
- Essays That Relate to Teachings in The Book of Mormon
- Observations
- Commentary, Compendium, & Observations Index

Compendium
Volume Five

- Compendia Index
- Essays That Relate to Teachings in The Book of Mormon
- Observations
- Commentary, Compendium, & Observations Index

The Book of Mormon summons us to trust in God's divine design rather than putting all of our marbles in the basket of devilish doctrines. It invites us to believe that our lives are "fairy tales waiting to be written by the hand of God." (Hans Christian Anderson).

Compendium
Volume Six

- Compendia Index
- Essays That Relate to Teachings in The Book of Mormon
- Observations
- Commentary, Compendium, & Observations Index

Compendium
Volume Seven

- Compendia Index
- Essays That Relate to Teachings in The Book of Mormon
- Observations
- Commentary, Compendium, & Observation Index

Compendium
Volume Eight

- Introduction
- Hebrew Poetry in The Book of Mormon
- Synonymous Parallelism
- Antithetical Parallelism
- Synthetic Parallelism
- Climactic Parallelism
- Chiasmus
- Book of Mormon Scriptures Illustrating

Observations
Volume One

- 550 Observations

Observations
Volume Two

- 550 Observations

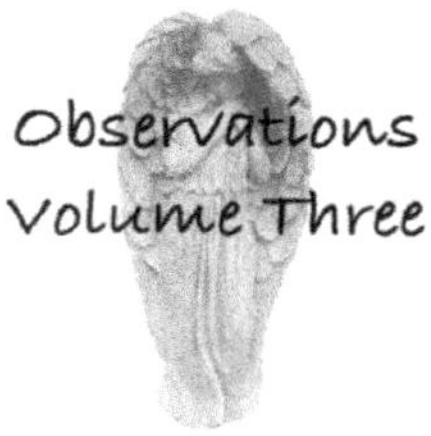

Observations
Volume Three

- 550 Observations

Observations
Volume Four

- 550 Observations

As we undertake an investigation of The Book of Mormon, we sometimes ask ourselves if it easier to be slothful, and harder to be upright. Is it the easier way out to be swayed by secular humanism, and harder to be faithful to the spirit of revelation?

Observations Volume 5

- 550 Observations
- Commentary, Compendium, & Observations Index

Observations Volume 6

- 550 Observations
- Commentary, Compendium, & Observations Index

If we want
to open our hearts to
The Book of Mormon, we
must begin by our taking
a few confident steps into
the darkness. Only then,
will its spiritual strong
searchlight illuminate
the way that leads
to our journeys'
end.

A Book of Mormon Commentary
Volumes One - Three

Compendia
Volumes One - Eight

Observations
Volumes One - Six

www.ingramcontent.com/pod-product-compliance
Lightning Source LLC
Chambersburg PA
CBHW061400010526
44107CB00012B/1004